T0209109

OUR
LONG
ROAD
HOME

authorHOUSE®

AuthorHouse™
1663 Liberty Drive
Bloomington, IN 47403
www.authorhouse.com
Phone: 1 (800) 839-8640

Published by AuthorHouse 12/04/2019

ISBN: 978-1-7283-3870-5 (sc)
ISBN: 978-1-7283-3868-2 (hc)
ISBN: 978-1-7283-3869-9 (e)

Library of Congress Control Number: 2019920179

DEDICATION

This book is Dedicated to my daughter Jae Alexia Jackson. You were far too young to understand the impact your survival story had on many people. Being only two when you started your journey, you had no clue of how what God was doing for you was blessing so many others. I wrote this book for them. But more importantly, I wrote this book for you. I wrote it for you because, when you're well into that long life I pray that God will allow you to live, you'd be able to look back and share in precise detail how strong you were and how valiant of a fighter you were. This is the least of what I owe you for teaching me how to live a life of gratefulness and purpose.

Don't let anybody fool you into believing that trials and tribulations won't cause you to worry about what the end will be. But God just spoke some words to me that I pray blesses some of you. God Will Handle the Problem ... all you gotta do is Handle the Process. Handling the Process becomes so much easier when we understand that there's a PURPOSE behind EVERYTHING that God ALLOWS. Put the Problem in Your Rear View Mirror... see it but don't make it your focus. Put the Purpose in your Windshield ... focus on it intently and make it bigger than your problem. Keep that in mind second by second ... minute by minute ... day by day ... and before you know it, the Process will be over, and GOD will have handled the problem.

Unedited post to Facebook on June 11, 2018

CHAPTER 1
Our Lives Were Perfect

On June 10, 2018, our lives took a shift none of us were prepared for and presented my family with a test that would leave us at a breaking point. It was a beautiful Sunday morning. I woke up feeling extremely blessed to be alive and a witness to all that was happening. Until this point, 2018 had arguably been one of, if not, the greatest year of my life. So much of what I had been praying for was coming to pass. Dreams I had dreamt for years were becoming reality and all of the seeds I had sown, hoping for a harvest, were materializing right before my eyes. It had been an amazing year so far, and I didn't mind testifying about what God was doing and giving Him all of the glory. There was no doubt in my mind that if it were not for Him, all of the great things wouldn't have been occurring. As a pastor and spiritual leader, I encouraged anybody who would listen to me to exhibit the kind of faith I had in God so they, too, could experience the kinds of miracles, signs, and wonders I was experiencing. I declared 2018 as "The Year Under an Open Heaven."

One of the great things happening in my life was that I was finally getting to watch my wife, Dee, blossom into the woman she was always destined to be. During our marriage, she had stood in the background as I progressed through my life goals. By June 10, 2018, Dee had begun to shine like never before. All of her laboring in the background had finally polished her up and prepared her for placement in the forefront. In 2017, she'd been named the interim county administrator in Gadsden County, the same county that we grew up in. Later that year, she was unanimously voted in as the permanent county administrator, making her the first woman in the county's 200-year history to hold such a position. Watching how she supported me when she was in the background, taught me my role as I took my place in the background. On June 10, 2018, I couldn't have been happier for her, and all she was accomplishing in her career.

Throughout this book, you will see many signs of the hand of God moving in various situations; Dee's appointment is one of those moves of God. It was remarkable because though she had been on the county administrator's "A" team, she had never pursued the county administrator's position. Not only had she never sought the county administrator's position, but she wasn't even next in line for the promotion or fifth in line for that matter. It was as if her appointment and promotion were in some way, God fulling promises He had made to her. That's significant because, until this date, it seemed like this was going to be the year God fulfilled all of His promises to us. In February 2018, we were blessed to be able to purchase our dream home. After struggling from the pits of financial obscurity, where we couldn't even afford to purchase a mobile home when we got married twenty years earlier, we were now living in a sprawling residence with all of the amenities a family that started in a one-bedroom shack could appreciate. This, too, was evidence that the hand of God was moving in our lives.

In March 2018, we witnessed the favor of God strike again. Five years earlier, Dee and I had walked out on faith and left a church we'd led for thirteen years. We founded Destiny Church Tallahassee in 2013 and built it ourselves, alongside a few faithful people who believed, as we did, that the primary mission of the Church wasn't to just "have church," but to be a blessing to those in need, even those outside the four walls of our gathering place. We had been renting a facility for four years, blessing families not only with the Word of God, but thousands of pounds of food, clothing, and other household goods when a chance encounter blessed us with a property owner, who believed so greatly in our mission that he helped us purchase the building he was trying to sell. Without God touching this man and his family's heart, there would have been no way a ministry the size of ours, with limited financial resources, could have even fathomed purchasing. We were being blown away by all of these major blessings. There was no doubt that God's hand was upon our lives.

But more important than any of the material things we had been blessed to acquire, I woke up on June 10, 2018, feeling beyond blessed that our family was still together and stronger than ever after all of these years. Our twenty-one-year-old son Jaelen, was off in college at Florida A & M University, making us proud and on the verge of graduating with a dual degree in business administration. Our nineteen-year-old daughter Joana, was following in her brother's footsteps, attending the same school, and pursuing the same degrees. Our thirteen-year-old son Jan, who is the smartest of our kids, but a little more rambunctious than his siblings, was excelling academically and athletically. And Jae, our little two-year-old daughter—yes, I said two; though born prematurely, weighing only 4.1 pounds at birth, was healthy, happy, and growing like a weed. This baby had become and still is the apple of each of our eyes. I couldn't have been happier. I couldn't have been more satisfied with where I was in life. My family was strong, our financial situation was secure, and our future was as bright as it had ever been. On June 10, 2018, our lives were perfect. But June10, 2018 was also the day that everything changed.

CHAPTER 2
And Then the Bomb Dropped

I woke up first, like I normally do, got a cup of coffee, and started laying out my clothes to wear to church that day. After mulling over which tie I should put on, I started waking up the rest of the family. As the rest of us got dressed and entertained each other with small talk, Jae slept peacefully. We always let her sleep until we were fully dressed for two reasons. First, she was not a morning person and normally woke up agitated by the fact that we woke her up. And secondly, she always demanded our full attention. Getting dressed while Jae was awake, always proved to be a bit challenging. So, we let her sleep.

When she finally woke up, Jae was uncharacteristically in a great mood. And, per our custom, everybody in the house rushed to her bedside to see who was going to get the morning's first hug and kiss from her. On this morning, it was Dee. She picked Jae up with a hug and repeated kisses like only a mother could give. As Jae gleamingly smiled, we each took turns loving on her before Dee whisked her away for a morning bath.

As Dee bathed her, she noticed a huge knot on Jae's left shoulder blade. Dee called me into the bathroom to ask if I knew how she might have developed such an obvious deformity. I replied that I hadn't noticed the swelling the day before. With a puzzled look, Dee said she hadn't noticed it, either. Seeing this was quite odd; we had no clue where it could have come from. Jae wasn't exhibiting any obvious signs of pain. When we touched and pressed against the swollen area, she never even flinched. Jae was unfazed by what was now causing us anxiety.

Dee placed Jae on our bed and disappeared into the closet to get Jae's clothes, or so I thought. But after she didn't come out of the closet for an extended period, I walked in to see what she was doing. Dee was sitting on the floor, holding her phone. I assumed she was responding to an email or text; I'd later find out she was doing exactly what I was about to do. As she sat in the closet on her phone and Jae sat, all giggly, on our bed watching *Sesame Street* reruns, I grabbed my phone and searched WebMd, trying to figure out what could have caused the huge swelling to develop overnight on our baby's shoulder. What I read floored me. The first thing that popped up was an explanation saying something to the effect that if the swelling was accompanied by swollen glands around the neck, it might be a sign of cancer. I immediately dropped my phone as my heart raced and rushed to the bed to examine Jae's neck. Sure enough, I saw swelling there, too. I was mortified. I was scared into disbelief. I rejected that thought by saying to myself, "Naw, that ain't what it is. That can't be what it is."

As I frantically paced around the bedroom, I noticed that Dee was still in that closet. So, I looked in to see what was keeping her so long. I didn't know how to tell her what I had just seen, but I wanted to be in her presence. Just being around her always had a calming effect on me. I hoped when she emerged from the closet, she would have found this swelling to be nothing more than a minor issue that could be solved with a quick visit to the doctor's office. But when I looked into that closet, a woman I had always depended on for her strength and glossy-eyed positive view about life and its trials, had crumbled with her face between her knees. As I inched closer, I realized she was weeping. I got down on my knees beside her and asked what was wrong. She couldn't seem to muster the words. But as I knelt, rubbing her back, trying to encourage her, I saw what she had seen.

As we sat on the closet floor, through tears, she said, "I just want my baby to be okay."

I rushed to think of every reason that could explain away what we had seen on WebMD. I said that Jae had probably fallen at my mother's house, or she may have been bitten by an insect last night, or maybe she had dislocated her shoulder playing with her brother. I spewed out enough plausible explanations that I started to see hope in Dee's eyes.

"You're probably right," she said. And just like that, the strong, glossy-eyed, positive thinker I knew was back. "Let's go to church, and when we leave, we will take her to the doctor. She's going to be just fine." I felt better. Dee seemed to feel better. With a glimmer of hope that all would be well, we finished getting Jae dressed, and we went to church.

Church was great. As always, Jae stood and sang along with the praise team, clapping her hands as she stood next to her mother, periodically looking up at Dee as if to gain her approval. As I preached, she shouted, "Amen!" just like her grandmother Lessie, who she'd normally opt to sit with when I got up to preach. This child had always been a worshipper. She loved going to church; she loved praising God, which would be something that proved pivotal in how we approached God concerning her in the days and months ahead.

After we left church, we were all in such a great mood. We went out to dinner at a local vegan restaurant. Our church had just begun a no meat fast on June 1 with daily morning corporate devotionals and prayer. At the table, I told Dee we should wait until tomorrow to take Jae to her doctor, instead of taking her to urgent care that day. But as we ate, I noticed the once hopeful gleam in Dee's eyes was now fading. She seemed worried. She seemed anxious. So, I said, "If it would make you feel better, we should just go today and have Jae checked out." She said, "That's what I want to do."

Without telling any of our family or friends, we left dinner and headed for urgent care, not knowing when we had left home that morning, we would not return for a long while. And when we did return, life as we knew it would be turned upside down. A bomb had just dropped in the center of our lives. We had no clue it was about to explode, nor did we know how devastating its effects would be.

CHAPTER 3
The Nightmare Begins

When we arrived at Capital Health Plan Urgent Care, I didn't want to go inside. My prayer was that they would go inside, come back a short time later with some medicine, and we'd head home to watch the swelling go down. But that's not what happened. After about an hour of waiting in the car, I walked inside and found Dee in a small room, sitting on a table, holding Jae as she slept. Dee told me that Jae had already completed one X-ray and that she had already been subjected to getting a catheter so that medical staff could get a urine sample. As we waited for the results of the X-ray and Urine sample, I started to feel the weight of what might be our reality. That weight got a little heavier when the doctor walked in with this unforgettable nervous look and ordered another X-Ray because the first one didn't definitively tell him the issue. That weight got even heavier when he walked back into the room, looking somberly after the second X-ray. What he saw was still inconclusive but had scared him enough that he ordered that we go to Tallahassee Memorial Hospital immediately. He told us that Jae could be examined by modern equipment, and we could get clarity on what was going on with her by going to the hospital.

We had been at urgent care from around 1:00 until 5:00 p.m. But we were no closer to an answer than we were before we left home. Though we were no closer to the answers we needed, we were closer to an emotional breakdown. Jae had already experienced a traumatic day. From watching her being painfully forced to endure having her temperature taken anally to standing by as she resisted being forced to stay still as she went back and forth through an X-Ray machine;

Dee and I were hurting over the fact that our baby girl had to go through so much. However, we couldn't show any of our mental anguish. Our mission was to make Jae as comfortable as possible in between what had to be uncomfortable procedures, during what had become an arduous process. Four hours later, we grabbed our baby and headed to the hospital as we'd been ordered. The only thing I wanted to do was take my baby home so that she could be in the place where I knew she'd be safe from whatever it was that was trying to attack her.

We arrived at Tallahassee Memorial Hospital on Medical Drive and were immediately escorted to the back to begin prepping for the ordered tests. Again, we had to hear our baby cry as they took her rectal temperature, gave her a catherization for a urine sample and stuck her repeatedly, trying to find a vein for an IV. Again, they put her through these monstrous machines that she was afraid of seeing. Once the tests were completed, we sat in a small, cold room, waiting for the doctor to come in with the results. We waited, and we waited, and we waited. Dee was holding Jae in her arms. It was around 11:00 p.m.; by now, and Jae was soundly asleep. Dee and I were wide awake, drained from the long day, and anxious about hearing the results of these tests. We stared listlessly into space, having no one else to lean on but each other, since we hadn't told anyone about what was going on. That's when the doctor walked in rather nonchalantly and precisely said, "I'm afraid that your daughter has cancer, and she needs to be transferred to Shands immediately."

As I'm writing this, I can still feel the heartbreak of that moment. Jae was sleeping in the safety of her mother's arms, completely oblivious to how seriously in jeopardy her little life was. As heartbroken as we were, neither of us cried. Maybe it was the sheer shock of the news we had received or knowing we had to be strong for our baby and each other. Whatever the reason, we didn't show any visible signs of emotion. I did, however, tell that doctor, "I'm taking her home tonight, and we will go to Shands in the morning." In my mind, I felt if I could only get my baby home, everything would be all right. As a father, I felt like I needed to protect her and Dee. The only place I knew how to do that was in the home I was so desperate to get back to, but we wouldn't be going home. That doctor replied to me in the same nonchalant and precise way he had spoken when he told us he was afraid that Jae had cancer, "We can't let you leave the hospital, sir. We've called an ambulance, and they will transport her within the hour."

That's when it all hit me. That's when I knew we needed somebody to lean on. The first person I called was my sister Marsha. When I told her the doctor just said he thought Jae had cancer, the only thing I heard on the other end of the line was the phone dropping and her weeping. I couldn't bare listening to my sister in that state; I was still in search of somebody we could lean on. So, I called my mother, and her response wasn't much better. Not only did this news crush Dee and I, now we were also forced to hear the evidence of how badly it crushed everyone close to us. Our children found out when Dee called her mother Sandra. They were spending the day with her. When Dee said the words Jae and cancer in the same sentence, her mother screamed the word cancer, our children heard that scream. I later found out that Joana, my oldest daughter, just ran out of the house and had to be found and consoled. Jaelen, my oldest son, was in Charlotte. We made it clear to our family that he shouldn't find this out until he returned in a few weeks.

I thought if we were headed to Gainesville, about two-and-a-half hours away, I'd have to go home to get us some clothes. I figured we'd at least need something to wear the next day. So, I did, and I drove like a bat out of hell, trying to make sure I was back before they loaded my baby into that ambulance. On the way home, I never cried. I was in a state of shock. I was moving, but I wasn't feeling anything. I was numb. Once I got home, I quickly packed a bag and was on the way out the door when Dee's mother arrived. She was bringing the kids home to get some clothes so that they could spend the night with her. As they walked into the house looking sad, I walked in behind them. I hugged them and told them that everything was going to be all right. My kids typically never express emotion. But on this night, they both looked broken and I felt their brokenness when they began weeping in my arms.

I needed them to be near me; so, I asked if they wanted to ride to Gainesville with me. My son declined, but my daughter said she wanted to go. Without another word being exchanged, we rushed out of the house, jumped in the car, and sped back to Tallahassee, praying to be there before they left with Jae in the ambulance. We got there just in time. I watched as they loaded a stretcher, carrying my baby into the ambulance. Dee rode with her, and I followed closely behind until we reached Shands Children's Hospital at the University of Florida in Gainesville around 2:00 a.m.

CHAPTER 4
The Long Uphill Road Ahead

When we arrived at Shands, Jae was rushed into the emergency room. They immediately begin prepping her for tests that would take place on the fourth floor in the Pediatric Cancer Unit. We were exhausted, sleepy, and grief-stricken, but there would be no sleeping for us. There was no time for us to feel sorry for Jae or ourselves. Everything and everybody around us were moving fast around us, preparing Jae to be examined and treated. Joe, one of the emergency room nurses comforted us and explained what we should expect for the next few days. He also told us that we'd be meeting Dr. Lagmay later that day, who he deemed to be one of the best in the world.

After a couple of uncomfortable hours in the emergency room, a team of nurses escorted us upstairs to our room. As we walked down the halls, I glanced into the rooms along the way, seeing all these other children hooked up to machines. I was scared more than I've ever been in my life. It seemed with every step I took and every glance into those rooms, the more afraid I became. I was in utter disbelief that we were even there. How could this be? How in the world could I wake up on a Sunday morning so happy about life and still be up early on the next morning, feeling such despair? That feeling of despair was crystalized when we finally reached our room, and I saw *Jae Alexia Jackson* on a name card plastered on the wall next to the door.

Timidly, we walked into the room. We got as comfortable as we could on a small green pullout bed — all four of us, including Dee, Jae, my oldest daughter, and me. Dee held the girls close; I stretched my arm across all of them and held them all. Fearful about our future,

I just wanted them close to me. I believed Dee felt the same way. After all we had been through on a day that never seemed to want to end, it felt good for it all to be over, if only for a little while. We drifted off to sleep around four o'clock. But before we could even begin to dream about a brighter day, we were awakened by a team of doctors around six that morning. Let me say, there's nothing more intimidating than waking up to six doctors, all specializing in the treatment of cancer. We were frightened by their presence, but in a way, we were also happy to see them. Their presence meant they were about to tell us what was wrong, and prayerfully, they'd be able to tell us how to fix it.

Led by Dr. Joanne Lagmay, one of the leading childhood cancer specialists in the country, they told us about their plan to assess the potentially cancerous area. I used the word potentially because, though the CAT scans in Tallahassee had revealed a mass that could be cancerous, there was no way of knowing for sure until they conducted a biopsy to declare a diagnosis.

They did, however, do some preliminary tests to assess her. The fact that outside of the large overnight growth on her shoulder, Jae didn't show any visible signs of being infected with this disease, was odd. The doctors did all kinds of manual tests, including pressing deeply into her stomach and legs to see if she was in any pain. They even tapped on her bones to see if she was in any pain. Nothing they did caused the slightest wince. They asked us had we seen any signs of pain like crying or immobility, but we told them we hadn't. Outside of a couple of issues any other baby might have, we hadn't noticed anything. They were puzzled by this. If she had what they thought she had, a tell-tell sign would have been pain, but she wasn't in any pain. Shortly after that, as we waited for the diagnosis, they started Jae on a medicine to prevent any further growth of the mass.

Around nine that morning, they came back to take her downstairs for the biopsy. One of the hardest things I had ever done was to let her go and hear her crying and screaming my name as she left. Following the biopsy, they brought Jae back to the room. Again, we found ourselves waiting for results. We had spent all day praying that they found nothing serious and were longing for the moment we could return home with our baby, free and clear of any life-threatening health issues. Neither of us had family histories of cancer; it just can't be. We waited all day for the doctors to come back and give us the results of the biopsy, but they never did.

Eventually, we fell asleep on that little green pullout, holding each other just like we had done the morning before. Around five or so, we were startled out of sleep again by this young female doctor who was undoubtedly kind, but very blunt. As she knelt quietly by our bedside, she whispered, "I'm so sorry to tell you. But your daughter does have cancer. It's a rare form that rapidly spreads ..." and that's all I heard her say. She was still talking; only I couldn't hear anything. I was in a darkened daze. Then, the tears I hadn't been able to shed begin uncontrollably rolling down my face. As she continued with all of the details about the kind of cancer it was, and which plans of action would be immediately taken, my arm that had clutched Dee and the girls, was drenched. I felt the tears of my wife, dripping on my arm as she sobbed uncontrollably.

I can't recall any of the other details she shared that morning. I do remember when Dr. Lagmay, who would be Jae's primary doctor on this journey, came in later that morning to affirm what we had been told earlier. Again, I drifted off into a daze when I heard the word cancer. But once she was done talking to us, I remember jumping out of bed and following her out of the room. Once outside, I had a one-on-one meeting with her; I had only one question that I needed answered. With tears streaming down, standing just outside of the room, I looked directly into her eyes, and asked, "Is my daughter going to live?"

Dr. Lagmay responded, "I don't know. I can't make any promises about whether or not Jae will live or die. But I'm an expert in neuroblastoma, which is the kind of cancer she's diagnosed with. I've been successful treating this kind of cancer before, and I assure you that I'm going to do everything in my power to save Jae's life." She didn't leave any room for doubt about promising whether my baby would live. She couldn't do that. What she did promise however, was that we had a long, uphill road ahead of us.

CHAPTER 5
I'll Deal with the Facts; You Deal with the Faith

At the time of Jae's diagnosis, I was forty-three years old. For the next four days after she was diagnosed, I cried more than I had cried in all of the days of my life combined. I couldn't stay in the room long, because every fifteen minutes, I felt the tears in my heart, trying to break through my eyes. I always left the room when I felt that way because, I never wanted Dee or Jae to be emotionally weakened by my emotional weakness. But not only did I never want to be in their presence when I cried, I didn't want to be present again when any doctor entered the room to talk about Jae's condition or treatment.

It wasn't that I was disengaged or didn't care. But for the first time in my life, there was something I didn't feel I could handle without breaking down. The process hadn't even begun, and I was already overwhelmed. If I was going to be as strong as I could for my child and family, I couldn't do that. So, every time a doctor walked into the room, I'd leave. I'd stay gone until I called back to the room to confirm with Dee that they had left. That happened a few times before Dee said she had noticed how I always left when the doctors came in. As she questioned me about my obvious absence, my eyes began welling up with tears. Hearing her ask why I wasn't there, made me feel like a weak man. I felt like I was letting her down by continuing to run away. When Dee noticed those tears, just beneath the surface, she pulled me into the bathroom.

She didn't say anything at first. She just held me tight while I cried like a baby on her shoulders. She told me, "It's okay to cry" and to "Let it all out". This girl I married all those years ago was proving once again, to be my rock during weary times. Grabbing my face, she started explaining why I kept leaving the room. She said, "I know how hard it must be for you to see Jae in this situation and how hard it must be to hear how bad it is. But that's why God put us together. You have always been strong in areas where I'm weak, and when faced with those times, I could always count on you to be my strength. This situation is no different. You be strong for me in the areas that I know I'm going to be too weak to handle, and I promise you, I'm going to be strong for you in the areas you're too weak to handle." She lifted my head off of her shoulders, looked into my eyes, and said, "I'll deal with the facts as long as you promise me that you'll deal with the faith." Those words proved to be profound and pivotal as we progressed through this process, because Dr. Lagmay was about to deliver news that I don't know how I would have handled had I known all of the facts at the time.

CHAPTER 6

Your Will Be Done

One of the most important things to figure out before cancer can be treated is the stage of the cancer. Understanding the stage of the cancer is crucial in determining if it's possible to treat the cancer, and if so, how aggressive the treatment needs to be for the desired outcome. After a battery of tests, Jae's doctors scheduled a meeting with us to share that information. Because we had already established an agreement that I wouldn't meet with the doctors to discuss any details, Dee headed into that meeting alone. She was comfortable with doing it, and I was confident she didn't need me to be present for what I thought would be a brief meeting. I assumed the meeting would end with doctors confirming the only thing I cared to know—that this was a treatable form of cancer, and a treatment plan had been established.

As minutes of waiting turned into hours, I grew nervous. I was in the hospital room with Jae and a few of our family members, anxiously waiting for Dee's return. I wasn't in a big rush to see her. Though I needed to hear what the doctors had said, I didn't know if I wanted to hear the news she would come back with. Whenever she returned, I knew that there would be some things that I would be looking for to tell me the story of what she had just heard. I needed to see her facial expression. I needed to see something in her body language, exuding the kind of confidence that would let me know she felt everything was going to be okay. But when she finally returned, I saw her approaching through the little glass window in the door. I could tell from her pale expression that whatever she had heard had shaken her.

Before she could enter the room, I scrambled toward the door to meet her. She needed me, and whatever she was feeling didn't need to be brought into a room full of people who had already proven they couldn't handle the kind of news she was undoubtedly about to share. I asked them to watch Jae while we took a walk to the hospital's courtyard. As we walked around the pristine grounds of the hospital, I asked Dee to tell me what the doctors said that scared her. She didn't answer that question directly, but she reminded me of the agreement we had already established. Though I pressed for more information, her words to me were, "I'll handle the facts; you handle the faith." The things she shared with me that day were the only things I cared to know; Jae had cancer, the doctors had come up with a treatment plan, and it was going to be okay. That's what I needed from her. I needed that assurance. I needed to be able to look in her face and feel like she felt everything was going to be all right, and that's exactly what she gave me.

I found out months later the kind of weight Dee had been carrying around. What she had refused to share with me that day was that our baby girl had been diagnosed with stage four, high risk, neuroblastoma. Jae's cancer had already spread throughout much of her body, including her lymph nodes and bones. She was covered in tumors from the neck down, with one the size of a grapefruit in her abdomen. Knowing what I know now about the severity of the cancer, and the other things I never knew because she was committed to our agreement, I can unequivocally say that Dee Jackson is one of the strongest women alive. But, at that moment, she was weak. It was my responsibility, as the person who was supposed to handle the faith aspect of this journey, to lead her through it.

I took her outside for a walk. We held hands; she started explaining some of the parts of the process we'd have to go through. She also said the doctors strongly advised that we stay away from the internet. They recommended we refrain from reading anything that could cause us any more stress and anxiety than we already had. Our orders were to focus on Jae's cancer, and nobody else's, because each case was different. They didn't want us fearing what could happen based on what anyone else had experienced.

I found a park bench, so we could sit for a minute and continue the conversation, but our conversation abruptly ended when Dee fell into my arms, crying and saying, "That's my baby up there, and she has cancer." Hearing her say those words shook me to my core. She was weak and needed me. As she got weaker, I got stronger. I begin encouraging her with the word of God. I said, "I believe that God is going to heal our baby. We have seen Him do things like this before in the lives of other people we know and have prayed for them. If He did it for them, certainly He will do it for us." I grabbed her hand and began praying. I prayed to God to strengthen her, and I prayed for God to heal Jae. I also gave God a reason to save our two-year old's life. I told God that Jae loved to praise and worship Him, and if He healed her body, He would be giving her a chance to glorify Him again. I gave God several reasons to save her. I told God if he saved our baby, we would release her to the world, under His authority, so she could be living proof in the earth that He was a way maker and miracle worker. But how I ended my prayer, prompted an uncomfortable conversation.

See, not only did I give God a reason to save Jae's life I also gave Him permission to have His way. I ended my prayer much like Jesus had when He was faced with great despair at the Garden of Gethsemane, where He said, "Lord, let Your will be done." That sounded like a reasonable way to end a prayer until I was forced to think, *What happens if it's God's will that our baby isn't healed?* And that's exactly what Dee asked me when I finished praying. Dee said, "I don't know if I could just give up that easy and submit to whatever God's Will is, especially knowing that God's will might not line up with ours." I understood the point she was trying to make. She wasn't doubting God's will; she was trying to box God into the answer she wanted. She's never told me this, but I believe she'd rather I not have prayed for God's will to done and focused all of my petitions on Jae's complete healing. I was holding her hands, looking into her eyes, and trying to convince her to say, "Lord, let Your will be done," with me. She continued to refuse until I brought something key to her remembrance.

I reminded her of Jae's birth; how she said God had shown her that Jae was going to minister to the world one day. I reminded her of all the days she had looked into that baby's eyes and repeated that prophecy. I also reminded her of the day we dedicated Jae's life to God before our family and friends, where we held her up before those people and told God that we were giving her back to Him and released her back into His hands. I said that it was easy to release her back to God when we knew we still had a measure of control over what happened in her life. But now that we knew there was nothing in our power we could do to save her, it was difficult to take our hands completely off.

We were at a place, as parents, where there was nothing we could do. We were powerless. Tylenol wasn't going to fix this. Holding her a little tighter wasn't going to fix this. Wishing she didn't have to go through this wasn't going to fix this. The money we had in the bank wasn't going to fix this. The influential friends we had weren't going to fix this. We were at a place demanding our complete dependence on God. Giving Him permission to have His way was not a white flag of surrender. No, I wasn't giving up. I was activating our faith. I was letting God know that whatever He decided to do, we trusted Him, even if that meant our daughter was taken from this earth. Dee wept a bit more, but she was nodding in agreement. When I asked her to say it with me one last time, she said, "Lord, let Your will be done."

CHAPTER 7
Job Was Healed When He Prayed for His Friends

S ince that fateful Sunday morning, we had been at the hospital for a few days. We had left home hoping for the best and hadn't been back yet. We were dealing with the heartbreaking and life-shattering news that our baby girl had cancer. We had gotten the diagnosis; we had gotten a treatment plan; and we had at least a yearlong, uphill journey ahead of us that may or may not save our daughter. The thoughts of *she may live* always encouraged us. But there were those days where the thoughts of *what if she doesn't?* terrified us. In the early stages of the process, those thoughts were more prevalent.

I encouraged Dee out of fear and doubt. Just as she was regaining her strength, I started losing mine again. The one thing about going through a journey that you need to understand is it's an emotional rollercoaster with many sharp dips and turns. One day, I felt encouraged and came up with the **#JaeSTRONG** mantra. That day, I was strong enough then to tell our family to, "Cheer up because Jae is strong, and she's going to ring that damn bell!" But then there were other days when I fell into deep depressive thoughts. I wasn't crying as much, but I wasn't talking or eating much, either. I started drastically shedding weight. My eyes were even sunken.

I'm sure Dee noticed the drastic decline in my emotional wellbeing. She didn't say anything about it until I backed out of my responsibility to lead the daily Devotional & Prayer Call that I'd initiated along with the corporate fast, just weeks before all of this happened. She asked, "Why aren't you doing the call?" I replied, "I just don't have it in me. I'm too weak. I don't have anything to share, so, I shifted that responsibility to other ministers at the church."

That's when she began calling forth the man of God in me that had retreated into suppression and was being buried by the present circumstances. Dee reminded me that she had seen me lay my hands-on people and pray for them on several occasions and watched them recover. She reminded me of the many times, in spite of what I was going through, how I rose to the occasion to inspire and encourage others.

Dee pounded her point home when she reminded me of the night I received a late-night phone call from the daughter of one of my members. That daughter told me that her mother was lying at the point of death. The family had been called in to say final goodbyes, and I was asked to come to the hospital to pray with her before she passed away. They were even told to start thinking about what funeral home to call to retrieve the body.

That night, I walked into that room and saw a woman lying lifelessly in her hospital bed. The doctor present said that she probably wouldn't make it to see another morning. It was then that I grabbed her cold hands and began praying for her. When I touched her hand, surprisingly, she squeezed mine, and tears rolled down her face. I had to believe with her that she could live. So, I prayed for her, and I asked God for a miracle. By the time that prayer ended, I was confident not only was she going to live through the night, but she was also going to leave that hospital soon. I walked out of that hospital room. I told her daughter and all the family that had gathered that her mother was going to live. My exact words were, "You can cancel funeral plans; she ain't going nowhere."

Some fifteen years later, that lady is still alive. More important than the fact that she's still alive is the fact that her testimony was alive in Dee's mind. She used that testimony to reinvigorate my spirit. Dee said, "You're a powerful man of God, and there's no way I can accept you being that powerful of a man of God for everybody else and not be that same man of God for your own family. I need you to snap out of it," Then, she reminded me of our agreement by saying, "I told you I got the facts, but I really need you to handle the faith."

Dee further stated, "I expect you to be back on that call, ministering and praying for others in the morning. You need to stop sitting around in the hospital room all day, doing nothing but licking your wounds and feeling sorry for yourself. I believe God sent us here for a reason and He placed you, the man of God, on this cancer wing at Shands—not just to pray our daughter's healing into fruition, but to also pray for all those other children and families, suffering along with us." She encouraged me to go into their rooms and lay my hands on them, too.

After that stirring pep talk, I started feeling better. I was encouraged by everything Dee said. One question she asked me, changed everything forever. She asked, "When did things turn around for Job after he lost everything he had?" I had to think about that. Though I've been to seminary and have degrees in theology, I had never been asked that question and had never explored the answer. So, I didn't know when or how things began turning around for Job. She respectfully let me think about it for another few seconds. When she realized I didn't know the answer, she told me about a Scripture she had recently read. That Scripture was Job, Chapter 42, verse 10. The verse says, "After Job prayed for his friends, the LORD restored his fortunes and gave him twice as much as he had before." That's when she grabbed my hands, looked into my eyes, and with a smile said, "Job's situation turned around when he prayed for his friends, and I believe our situation is going to turn around when you pray for these families here with us." That revelation set my soul on fire. I was finally ready to leave Jae's bedside and excited about all of the opportunities I had right there on that floor to do what I know God called me to do. I left everything I was feeling, and my child, in the hands of God. I went throughout the hospital doing what He had called me to do.

It was empowering and uplifting to go into the rooms of other suffering families to pray with them and be able to tell them that by faith, everything was going to be okay. Even though my daughter was in a hospital bed, freshly diagnosed with cancer, and with an uncertain life expectancy, I walked the halls of Shands looking for people I could minister to. Seeing the smiles on their faces and the hope my presence and prayers brought to them, pushed me past my despair into a place where I believed God like I never had before for miracles; not just to happen in my child's life, but for miracles to happen in each of their lives, too. Going into those other rooms also forced me into a state of gratefulness and made me thankful our situation was a good as it was.

I was thankful because I met some children who had been in the hospital for months, waiting for organ transplants. One day, I was asked via a Facebook message to come and pray for a young girl awaiting a heart transplant. She couldn't leave the hospital until she had that transplantation. She was just another child on another waiting list, hooked up to machines until someone else died so that she could have a chance at life. I prayed for that girl and her family. Before I left the room, her grandmother, who was there visiting, asked if I could go down the hall and lay my hands on another one of her granddaughters only a few doors down, suffering from the same condition as the girl I had just prayed for. If I wasn't thankful for anything else, I was thankful that my family didn't have two suffering children in the hospital.

I saw circumstances even worse than that. I met this one lady whose daughter was waiting to die because there was no cure for her condition. She said her daughter was eleven years old, had been in the hospital for a year, and would probably never leave again. Here I was bemoaning the fact that my daughter had to go through a yearlong uphill process, and I was meeting parents with children who didn't have treatment plans because their diagnoses were incurable or if they were curable, they had to wait an undetermined amount of time to get transplants. I walked back to my daughter's room many days, thanking God that our situation wasn't any worse than it was.

The lesson I learned from those encounters was that sometimes we have to look past how bad our situations are to see that things could be far worse than they are right now. The only way we can do that is to stop wallowing in our situations long enough to venture into a hurting world, where people need our hope. No matter what we're faced with right now, always remember that there's somebody, somewhere who would trade their shoes for ours in a heartbeat. I also found great joy and comfort in something else. God presented me with opportunities not just to pray for families, but on a few occasions, He provoked me to be an immediate blessing in the lives of people I encountered in those halls. It's always good to pray, but there will be some people we encounter who need what we already have in our hands.

One day I saw a lady crying and visibly distressed in the hospital atrium. I stood at a distance and watched her, considering how to approach her to ask if she needed prayer. Standing there, I overheard her talking to herself, looking at papers that undoubtedly were bills. "I don't even have enough money to eat, Jesus." God showed me that she didn't need prayer as much as she needed to eat that day. So, I walked over to her, opened my wallet, and gave her every dollar I had in it. It was only about twenty-five dollars, but she was grateful and looked upon me like was an angel sent from heaven. I felt as if I had wings and was being lifted over my struggles. It felt good to be a blessing to her.

There was another lady I encountered while standing in line to get one of Jae's prescriptions filled on the ground floor at the hospital pharmacy. I was about two people behind her. When it was time to pay for her medicine, I overheard the pharmacist saying that her insurance company had refused to pay for that particular medication, and the total was $64.09. She said that there was no way she could pay for it, shook her head, and began walking away. That's when God pricked my heart and gave me another opportunity to be a blessing. I walked to the front of the line. As she meandered nearby on the phone with someone, trying to borrow money I asked the pharmacist if I could pay for her medication. When she said I could, I took out my bank card and paid for it. The other people in line saw what I had done, and they allowed me to go ahead of them to get my prescription filled.

As I stood there waiting for my prescription to be filled, the pharmacist informed the lady that someone had paid for her medicine, and she could now pick it up. Overwhelmed with joy, she looked around, asking who had done this for her. I would have desired to remain anonymous, but the pharmacist told her that that I had done it. She walked up to me, thanked me, and asked me my name. I replied, "That's not important; just know that God loves you."

Dee's encouragement had set me on fire. I was praying for my friends and being a blessing to strangers. I later found out that every prayer I had prayed, and every good deed I had done was a down payment on the turnaround that was about to come.

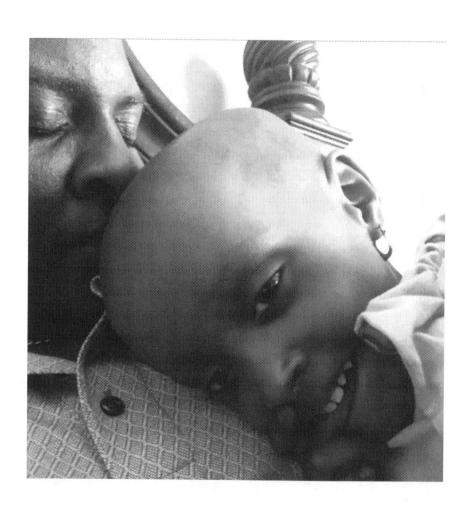

CHAPTER 8
Faith Over Facts

We aren't ever faced with anything in life that GOD thinks we can't handle. The difference between making it through and not making it through, boils down to whether or not YOU think what God thinks. Always focus on what God has already spoken. He won't burden you with anything you're not equipped to bear.
- Clarence Jackson

The first thing I noticed that had turned around for us was our state of mind. Jae still had cancer, and we hadn't even begun the first phase of treatment. But we were no longer mired in the depressive state that had gripped us when we first found out the news. Now I'd be disingenuous if I didn't state there were many days we battled emotionally. Certainly, there were moments I recall temporarily slipping into a funk. But by this time, our emotional roller coaster had less to do with whether or not we thought our daughter would live or die and more to do with whether or not we thought we could make it through this grueling process without breaking down. Even the doctors admitted that though this would be a difficult process for Jae, it was probably going to be more difficult for us.

Over time, I learned through conversations with other families going through the same situation, that the feelings of being overwhelmed and weary at times, were perfectly normal. However, the key to withstanding the pressures of traveling this long, difficult road was to keep our minds focused on the promises of God. We were in a place where we increasingly believed in God's abilities. We were walking in expectancy now and believing He was going to do what we were asking Him to do. If for no other reason, just because we were blessing others in the middle of our storm.

We had developed a radical faith. We had always been a family of faith. But something about our daughter being stricken with such a dreaded disease, pushed us deeper into our faith than we'd ever gone before. We knew if God didn't intervene, our baby's life expectancy would be in the hands of doctors; we wanted her life in His hands. So, we stuck to our radical faith, even if that meant defying the expectations of doctors with vast experience in treating Jae's type of aggressive cancer. We were walking heavily in our new-found Ephesians 3:20 anointing, which confirmed that God was able to do, "Exceeding abundantly above all that we ask or think." We had decided to always choose our faith over their facts. There were many times on this journey that those two thoughts clashed.

The doctors treating Jae were all wonderful. They were all highly regarded experts in their fields. We were thankful that we had been blessed to have our daughter treated by them. By no means will I ever discount the huge role they played in Jae's healing process, but they didn't do much faith talk. Their job was to bluntly present us with facts based on their experiences with treating this disease. Though we respected their expertise, we learned how to hear through what they were telling us so that we could stay focused on what God had told us. For instance, when they'd tell us about all of the side effects of chemotherapy or any other stage in this process, we'd already have gotten a word from God that Jae wouldn't have to experience all of that. We would sit and listen attentively to every word. As soon as they left the room, we'd look at each other and say, "She's not going to go through that."

I can vividly remember having one of those conversations with a doctor. When she finished talking to us, Dee blurted out, "That's not going to happen to Jae." Normally, we'd wait until they had left the room before we started our faith talk. This time was different.

The young doctor heard what Dee said, because she hadn't quite exited the room. She turned around and walked back over to Dee as she sat on the side of Jae's bed. The doctor knelt in front of Dee and said that she knew as a mother, she didn't want to see her child go through any of these things, but as a medical professional, who specialized in cancer treatment, she had to be honest and tell us these things were more than likely going to occur. Dee sat there and listened to every word she said and didn't respond. It was as if Dee was looking straight through her. When the doctor finished talking this time, Dee said again, but this time to her face, "That's not going to happen to Jae."

Dee's rejection of what the doctor said was born out of her desire to not see Jae go through these things. We had prayed about it, and God had shown us that Jae was going to sail through this process with minimal side effects. I observed Dee getting a little upset because the doctor didn't affirm her belief that Jae would be spared from all of these side effects. She was looking into space with a determined glare and saying, "God, they don't believe yet." Then she prayed for God to do something so miraculous for Jae during this process that even doctors, who restrained themselves from talking about faith, would have to admit it was God who had healed her. What Dee had just done was given God another reason to heal Jae. She was saying, "God, I don't just want you to heal my daughter because I want her to live; I want you to heal my daughter so that people will know that You live."

Our prayer life went into overdrive. We prayed over her Jae morning, noon, and night. We prayed over her before and after she received any medication. We even had a prayer handkerchief given to us by her godparents, Pastors Gerald and Judy Mandrell; we laid it on her every time she drifted off to sleep. The doctors were doing their job, and we thanked God for everything they were doing. We were on our jobs, too, and our family and friends were on theirs as well. Our job was to focus on what God could do and to never stop believing the report of the Lord, no matter how bad things got and no matter what the doctors said. We concluded the doctors didn't have to believe what we believed, as long as we were steadfast in our belief.

We were foolish enough to believe that as she slept, God was healing her body before the first drop of chemotherapy ever hit her veins. We were foolish enough to believe God was strengthening her little body so that she could withstand every blow this process threw at her. Our faith was strong. We were putting our faith to work. Soon, we would have to face some facts requiring every bit of faith we had.

CHAPTER 9

Momma Never Told Me There Would Be Days Like This

Toward the end of our initial stay in the hospital, we finally learned everything this process would entail. We were on our way home for the first time since we'd found out this devastating news and getting prepared for the journey ahead. We were about to face the fact that the life we had left at home over a week ago was no longer the life we had. Our lives had been shattered and forever altered by this cancer diagnosis. We also had to deal with the knowledge that for the next year of our lives, our sweet baby girl was about to be introduced to more pain and suffering than she'd ever had in her short life. That pain and suffering would be necessary for her healing. But the most painful part for me was that there was little I could do to alter that reality.

We were given the five phases of Jae's treatment plan. We were also given specifics about how those treatments could potentially affect her. Since she was only two years old and fragile in mind and body, the details we heard about this process could have broken us down.

First, Jae would have five rounds of chemotherapy. During this stage, she'd have to be hospitalized weeks at a time for daily chemo. We were warned that chemotherapy would be a rigorous process, where Jae could experience several debilitating side effects, including high fevers, fatigue, nausea, vomiting, easy bruising, bleeding, infection, loss of appetite, hair loss, and a few other things could potentially happen. In a nutshell, for the next few months, we were probably going to be taking care of a very sick little girl. On top of the scheduled hospital visits, we were also warned that if she ever got a fever, we'd have to rush her to a hospital within an hour. Medicines would have to be administered immediately and failing to do so could be fatal.

After four rounds of chemotherapy, she'd be scheduled for surgery. The type of cancer Jae was fighting had been proven to be resistant to chemotherapy. Because there was a great chance that a substantial amount of the tumors would still be present, this step in the process was crucial so that any remaining tumors could be surgically removed. There are risks associated with any surgery; the risks of this kind of surgery were especially high, considering where her tumors were and the fact that many of her internal organs could be compromised. What's significant about this is that Jae had tumors everywhere, including the visible one on her shoulder, internal growths on her pelvis, bones, and that grapefruit-sized tumor on her kidney the doctors feared was attached to her adrenal gland.

After surgery, Jae would have to go through a stem cell transplantation. During this step, doctors would attempt to harvest as many healthy cells from Jae's bone marrow as possible so that they could reintroduce them into her body. Giving her cells she had produced would be the desired approach. Having to use donor cells, would significantly increase the chance of her rejecting them, which would increase the chances of the stem cell transplantation being unsuccessful. If Jae couldn't produce enough healthy cells, she'd have to receive the cells of a donor. We were warned a transplantation would be another grueling process that could last forty-five days or more, and she'd have to be hospitalized the entire time. We were also informed that even after a successful transplantation, it was recommended we stay no further than thirty minutes from the hospital. This meant we'd have to be away from home for another extended period, away from our other kids, who were, no doubt, already being seriously affected by everything going on with Jae. Some of the side effects of a stem cell transplantation included high fevers, seizures, and mucositis. All of this was tough to handle from just thinking about what our two-year-old might face.

After the stem cell transplantation, Jae would go through radiation. Radiation would be a more targeted attempt to kill any remaining cancer cells. We were advised that radiation could last twenty-one or more days, depending on how much disease was still left in her body. During this stage in the process, we could expect her to suffer from fatigue. We may even see some skin changes, especially in the areas targeted by the treatment.

The final phase would be immunotherapy. It was explained as a cutting-edge cancer treatment recently added to the treatment of cancer patients to boost their natural defenses to fight cancer. It uses substances made by the body or in a laboratory to improve or restore immune system functions. It wasn't out of the norm for patients going through immunotherapy to experience fevers, shortness of breath, nausea, vomiting, and diarrhea. Hearing about all of these stages of the process was overwhelming enough. But realizing we were about to go through all of this was quite deflating. The thought of our two-year-old daughter going through all of this was a bit much for me to take in all at once.

One day, just before leaving the hospital to go home, Lauren Staley, an ARNP from Dr. Lagmay's office, walked into the room to talk to us. Over the past few days, I had heard all I needed to hear. Frankly, I was just ready to take my baby home. So, when she walked in, I walked out, and I stayed gone long enough for her to be gone when I returned, but she wasn't. When I opened the door, I noticed her still crouched down next to Jae's bed, talking to Dee. Before I could slip away again, she noticed me and asked that I come back and talk for a minute. She promised she didn't want to talk to me about anything relating to Jae. Instead, this time, she wanted to talk to me about me.

Lauren, as we'd grow to affectionately call her, asked a question that would eventually give my faith some roots. She explained how she had noticed shifts in my mood. She asked, "Is there anything that I can do to help you get through this process?"

Initially, I replied, "I'm fine. I don't need anything." But I quickly changed my mind and asked, "Are there any other families going through this process who wouldn't mind talking to us and sharing their experiences." Before she could answer that question, Dee interjected with some specifications to my request. She said, "We don't just want to talk to anybody; we want to talk to families who have had children battling the same kind of cancer that Jae has." Dee added that she hoped there would be somebody we could talk to who had completed the process. Lauren's eyes lit up. She smiled and said, "I know two families who I'm sure would be glad to talk to you." She asked us to give her a few days to contact them to see if they would agree to speak with us, and she would get back to us.

CHAPTER 10

*Strangers Become Family When
We Find Them in The Valley*

After seven days in the hospital, we were finally headed home. It was Father's Day, and I remember the drive home. I felt like I couldn't have gotten a better gift than for my daughter to be released and for us to finally be headed home to be with the rest of our family. We had just been through the worst stretch of days we'd ever had in our lives. We had been shell-shocked. Our lives had been rocked. We wanted nothing more than to be at home around the people who loved us most. Our family and friends had prepared an extravagant homecoming for us. They'd prepared our favorite dishes and had gifts ready to give to Jae.

Driving into our yard and seeing all of their faces, celebrating our return was one of the greatest feelings I'd ever had. It felt good to be back home around our family and friends. I remember taking a short walk through the woods in my backyard, looking at all of the beautiful greenery and being thankful I wasn't staring at those dull hospital room walls. We would have to head back to the hospital again soon, but nothing was going to stop the joy flooding our hearts. But something did.

After a few hours of great food and family fun, one of our family members suggested that everyone should start preparing to leave. She had made this suggestion because she was sure we were worn out and wanted us to try and get some rest. Everybody, including me, agreed to that plan. We were tired, and indeed, in need of some rest. Everyone started trickling out, and we said our goodbyes, still on cloud nine about being home. As the last person left the house, Dee and I walked with them outside and stood on the front porch, hugging each other, waiting for them to get into their car and drive away. When their car disappeared from our view, we smiled at each other, embraced a little tighter, and took long sighs of relief. However, it wouldn't be long before those smiles were smeared by our tears.

Those tears seemingly came out of nowhere, and they weren't happy tears. As we held each other on that porch, we sobbed like a couple who had experienced the loss of a loved one. It was truly a sad sight. I didn't have any encouraging words for Dee and I didn't want any encouraging words from her. I was walking away, without saying a word, heading to find a place where I could go ahead release all of what I was feeling in private.

I'm sure Dee shares my sentiment when I say that this was the moment where reality started to really sink in. That's the moment when we knew our lives had changed forever. That's the moment when we thought about the fact that just a week ago, everything was perfect in our lives, but now here we were, and everything we knew about our lives had been shattered. This was the moment when bitterness shined brighter than my faith. I looked up toward heaven with tear-stained eyes, toward the same God I had just proclaimed to have so much faith in, asking Him how in the world could He let something like this happen to my baby. For those who might question my faith, let me be clear. I don't care how much faith you have; there will be some moments when the reality and the gravity of what we're going through crushes you. I was crushed. My daughter had cancer and being home didn't change that fact.

I sat around the house for a few days, feeling as sorry for myself as I had when we first found out Jae had cancer. I was still praying, but I was still in pain. I still had faith; not necessarily because I wanted to, but at this point, faith was all I had. Yet, my outlook changed drastically when my phone rang from a number I didn't recognize. Now I rarely answered calls I didn't recognize. Considering this call could be from a doctor or insurance company, I reluctantly answered. On the other end of the line was a man with a strong country drawl. I didn't know who he was. By the sound of his voice, I figured he had to be white and country. He said, "Hello, Mr. Clarence, this is John Driggers."

This was the call I had been looking forward to answering. John was the father of a little girl we had heard so much about. She had just finished her uphill journey, battling the same kind of cancer Jae had. If anyone could help us through this, it would be John and his family. I needed him, too. As a father, he must have understood everything I was going through. I needed to know how he had made it through this. I also needed to know what I should be expecting on this journey. Without knowing one thing about me, other than the point that my daughter had just been diagnosed with the same kind of cancer his daughter had, John Driggers, begin ministering to me like I was his brother. He had just come out of the valley; he voluntarily climbed back down in to shine his light onto our dark path to make sure we would come out of the valley, too.

John was, and still is, a great inspiration in my life. We've subsequently spent many days together. He and his beautiful family were a consistent presence when we were at the hospital. We've even been blessed to invite them into our home. Dee and I will always be grateful for his testimony and all of the time he and his family spent making sure we stayed encouraged. From that day, John walked me through every step of the process. When it got dark, he and his wife Jennifer were there encouraging us. When we saw the light at the end of the tunnel, they were there celebrating with us. When we called and asked them to pray, not only did they pray, they also enlisted the same prayer warriors who had prayed them through to pray us through. But there's one piece of advice John gave me that rings in my ears even now. I can hear him saying, with that country twang of his, "Mr. Clarence, that little girl is about to go through a lot. Make sure she smiles every day."

I'd later meet another father who had a daughter just a few months ahead of us in the same process. We had heard about their story, too. But after befriending John, I had all the support I needed; and I was hesitant about meeting him.

One day, as I stepped on the elevator, heading to my daughter's room, I saw this man I had seen around the hospital before. But this time, he was decked out from head to toe in clothes and shoes bearing the hashtag **#BrookeStrong**. I asked if his name was Trevor, almost at the same time as he asked me if my name was Clarence. The rest is history. Trevor Dunn, a tall, slim, hippy looking fellow; because he had made a vow not to cut his hair until his daughter was declared cancer free, became my brother. His family became my family. And like John, he became a huge player in how we navigated through this process.

Sometimes the things that make us feel the worst...turn out to be among the Greatest Blessings of Our Lives. In the middle of Trial and Triumph is where many of us give in to the pressures of the process. But what's to come is so much better than what's been. There's a HUGE Victory on the other side of your fears. You're stronger than you think you are ... You'll get through it.

Unedited post to Facebook on July 7, 2018

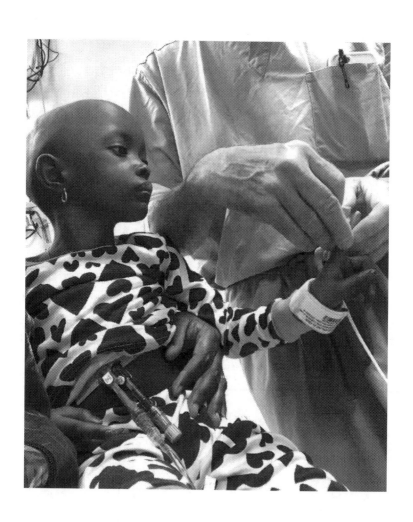

CHAPTER 11
Let's Get Ready to Rumble

After talking to John, the morning we left for Shands to begin Jae's first round of chemotherapy, my faith was strong again, my spirits were high. I was fired up and ready to fight this thing. Dee was much stronger and more hopeful, too. She had been regularly talking to Jennifer, John's wife. Dee was also ready to begin this fight. We woke up around five that Monday morning and loaded the car for the two-and-a-half-hour trip to Gainesville. We had to be there by nine. We left home around six to make sure we had ample time to get there and get checked in.

Just as we left the house, I looked in the rearview mirror and saw Jae asleep in her car seat. Seeing her sleeping peacefully and knowing she had no clue she was being driven to a hospital to begin a painful process, made my heart ache. The first thought that ran through my mind was, *My baby should be getting dressed to go to daycare like every other kid her age, but instead, here we are taking her to a hospital so harsh chemicals can be pushed through her veins.* I continued thinking, *This poor baby doesn't even know she's about to be introduced to a level of pain she never knew was possible.* That was a horrible thought, especially knowing there would be nothing I could do to ease her discomfort. But those thoughts didn't stop me from driving. I knew what she needed, and she was going to get it, even if that meant she had to go through pain. I was prepared for this. I was determined to be strong because this treatment had an assignment, and that assignment was to kill every cancerous cell in her body.

When we got to the hospital for check-in, Jae started noticing that something wasn't right. We saw her beginning to get a bit uncomfortable with her surroundings. She had been to this hospital before and she, undoubtedly, remembered the pain she had endured when she was there the last time. Dee and I did what we could to calm her down; including letting her watch kid videos on our cell phones. Whether she liked it or not, she was on the verge of the biggest fight of her life. As they escorted us to our room, it was as if we were trainers, leading a prizefighter into the ring. We encouraged her with every step saying, "You got this, Jae. You're a strong girl." We were confident and had every intention of winning this fight. But first, we had to win this round.

We sat in the hospital room for what seemed like forever, anxiously waiting for a nurse to come to start the process. Watching Jae being hooked up to all of those tubes had always been a challenge for me. This time, I couldn't wait for them to come in and connect her. After a while, a nurse came into the room. She smiled and said, "The treatment is about to begin."

All the talking we had been doing stopped. The TV was on, but I couldn't hear it. The room had been drained of all its electricity. This was a sobering moment. The room was so quiet and still that I heard Dee taking deep breaths. We had already planned that when the chemo started flowing, we were going to begin praying. So, when those chemicals started flowing through her veins, we laid our hands on our sweet baby girl and prayed, as she calmly rested on her bed.

We prayed for three specific things. The first thing we prayed for was that Jae wouldn't experience any of the side effects we were advised to expect. This specific prayer included room for God to allow side effects if He wanted to. But even if He allowed side effects, we asked that He strengthen Jae so that she would be able to withstand them. We also prayed that God would work in conjunction with the chemotherapy to produce better than expected results and to expedite her healing. We had already been informed of how resistant this type of cancer could be. So, we asked God to increase the shrinkage with every dose of chemotherapy. We asked God to shrink that cancer every time we prayed.

The last thing we prayed for was that God would completely heal Jae. We wanted Him to show Himself mighty to the world and show unbelievers how great He was. We wanted God to know that if He chose to heal Jae, she would be living, breathing, tangible evidence of His miracle-working power. We didn't know exactly what would happen next, but we believed something good was about to come out of this.

We attentively watched Jae's every move, trying to see how she was reacting to the chemo. Only we didn't notice any change in her. She was just as bubbly and vibrant as she had always been. We surmised that surely, after a few more hours of this, she would begin to slow down or feel some pain. But after the first day of chemo, we didn't see any signs that Jae was having any complications or side effects. Day two and three went by, and we still didn't see any signs of any adverse effects. Other than a few episodes of vomiting, which she always bounced right back from, this baby didn't seem fazed by the chemotherapy. On day four, Dr. Lagmay walked in and evaluated Jae. Noticing how strong she appeared and how resistant she had been to side-effects, she said, "This girl is a rock star. If I didn't know any better, I wouldn't even think she was going through chemotherapy."

Before we left to go home after the first round was over, this same doctor told us Jae had done amazing. What we were witnessing was not normal. Her exact words were, "This girl is going to breeze through this process." Jae proved to be STRONG, and God proved that He still heard and answered our prayers.

CHAPTER 12

In Between Rounds

Preparing to head home, we were a bit nervous about what would happen once we arrived there, especially knowing we wouldn't have any doctors or nurses to help us if something went wrong. We had been advised there would be lingering effects of the chemo and to especially be on the lookout for fevers. Due to the weakness, the chemo would cause, we were also given a few assignments to ensure her immune system was supplemented while she was at home, including giving her this shot and a cocktail of oral medications.

Though we were thrilled with how well she handled the first round of chemo in the hospital, going home with all of these new instructions was a daunting proposition. We found that Jae had an extraordinary threshold for pain. Normally after a few days of nausea and vomiting, which she typically handled like a champ, Jae would get right back to her normal self. Throughout this whole process, we never really saw Jae sick to the point where she lost weight or had to be in bed for long periods like we were told to expect. She kept a good appetite and stormed though many of those brief bouts with nausea. I often told people that if we didn't know Jae had cancer, it would be hard to believe. For the most part, she had a normal existence. But there were some tough moments in between hospital stays.

One of the toughest things for her to endure and for us to do, was to administer this particular shot every day. It was a drug called Neupogen and it was ordered to be given after each round of chemo to help fight infection. Neither of us had ever even used a needle before. But we were now forced into deciding who would be the one to take primary responsibility for administering that shot. Dee admitted she didn't want to do it, so I volunteered. That's how we rolled; in the areas where I was weak, she was strong. In the areas where she was weak, I stepped up. This was my moment to step up, so doing the shots became my responsibility. This required a team effort, though, and the first thing I had to learn how to do was give the shot.

One of the nurses taught me how to use the needle, just before we left the hospital, and my oldest daughter stepped up to be my test dummy. After practicing on my Joana, who bravely bore the pain of having needles pierce through the soft tissue of her arms and legs, I was finally confident I could handle this job. The tricky part would be how we would get Jae to sit still long enough for me to do it.

Waking up that first morning, knowing I had to give Jae this shot, made me apprehensive for two reasons. I wanted to do it right because her health depended on me doing it right. The second reason I was nervous was because giving her this shot would require her to go through some pain. But this wasn't just any pain. For the first time in her life, she would experience pain that I, me, her daddy would inflict upon her. I kept thinking that she's probably going to change her view of me. It was highly possible she'd no longer see me as the man who hugged, kissed her, told her how beautiful she was, and protected her. After all of these shots, I felt like she was probably going to associate my presence with pain and think of me as the man who brought her discomfort. I was a nervous wreck, but the time to do it was not. I had no choice but to do it. She needed me to do it. So, I just did it.

I'll never forget the first shot I gave her. Jae sat on the bed, watching Sesame Street. I washed my hands, put on my gloves, got the medicine from the refrigerator, and juiced up the needled. I called out to Dee and said I was ready. She grabbed Jae and brought her to me. Dee held her in her arms and tried to explain to this two-year-old that what was about to happen was necessary. As I inched closer with the needle in my hand, Jae lost it. She screamed at the top of her lungs as tears dripped down her face. She squirmed so fiercely that Dee had to wrap one of her legs around her body to try to control her movement. After several minutes of strongly fighting against receiving this shot, Jae weakened to the point where Dee could control her to be still enough for the shot. Dee closed her eyes and said, "Go ahead and do it." With tears in my eyes, I did.

When that needle pierced her thigh, she screamed, "Oh, no! No owies! No owies!" She had learned "No owies" from nurses at the hospital saying that to ensure her what she was about to go through wouldn't cause any pain. But here she was at home with her momma and daddy, and she was feeling owies. We just held her, kissed, and reassured her that we loved her. We had to go through this exact ritual almost every day for months. It never got any easier to give her the shot, and it never got easier for her to take it.

Another thing we had to get used to was taking her temperature. We had been informed of the risks of fevers. We knew how crucial it was for us to identify them and get her treatment within an hour if she ever had one. Not being vigilant considering this was a life or death proposition, and we weren't taking any gambles. To be prepared for if and when a fever came, we had a bag already packed. If her temperature reached 100.4 degrees, we had an iron-clad plan to exit the house and shoot to the hospital.

During breaks we had between chemo treatments, we experienced many fevers. The first time it happened, we almost lost our minds. We were tripping over each other, trying to get to the car and rush Jae to the hospital. But over time, we learned to be calm about this part of the journey. It was normal for fevers to occur during this process and going to the hospital was more of a precaution than evidence that something had seriously gone wrong. The biggest issue of going through one of these episodes was that if tests were done, and they found low white blood cell counts accompanying the fever, Jae would have to go back to the hospital. Those visits would normally last three to four days, and even during these times, Jae never seemed sick. Going through a fever episode was always worse on us than it was on her.

CHAPTER 13
Noticeable Changes

Following a couple of rounds of chemo, we started noticing some changes. The first visible change we noticed was that Jae had begun losing her hair. We were forewarned this was going to happen, so we thought we were prepared for when that day finally rolled around. Dee had already started buying headbands and hoods and researched wigs little girls could wear while going through chemotherapy. But nothing could have prepared us for the actual moment we saw her beautiful curly hair departing. I started noticing her hair loss before Dee did. It started to shed during the second round of chemotherapy; during a visit when Jae and I were alone as Dee stayed behind for work.

Several mornings while I was wiping Jae down, lotioning her body, getting her dressed for the day, I noticed her hair matting up. This was a dead giveaway the shedding was about to begin. Yet I never touched it. I wanted her hair to remain on her head as long as it could, and preferably, long enough for us to get back home to her momma. But one morning, there was a patch of hair so matted down in the front of her head that I couldn't help but pull it out because it was only hanging on by a few threads of hair. I put that wad of hair in a little plastic bag; I wouldn't dare throw something away that had been a part of her. Each morning after this, I woke up next to her and saw clumps of hair laying in the bed beside her. I just picked up those wads of hair as well and placed them in the bag.

By the time we were released and ready to head home, much of the hair on the top of Jae's head was gone. Just before leaving the hospital, I took a bandana off of a bear that one of the nurses had given Jae and tied it around her head. Since I had started to notice her hair falling out, I wouldn't let her get close to a mirror. Even at two years old, she loved her hair. Once she saw that much of it was gone, she'd probably have a hard time understanding why she looked so drastically different. I didn't tell Dee, either. She knew this day was coming and was sensitive to the idea of Jae losing her hair. I wouldn't even let her see Jae's head when we video chatted on the cellphone.

When Jae and I left the hospital, I brought her home with that little orange bandana wrapped on her head. She seemed to love the idea of having it and smiled all the way home, not knowing the only reason she had on that bandana was because I didn't want her to see what was under it. When we got home, Dee was standing outside, waiting for us to pull into the driveway. She was happy we were home. Before we got into the house, I explained that Jae's hair had begun falling out. I tried to explain how her head looked. I said, "I want you to be prepared for what you're about to see so that you'll be ready to help me deal with whatever reaction Jae has to what she will eventually see herself in a mirror."

The moment of truth had arrived. Dee was itching to see how Jae's head looked. As she untied the bandana, more hair fell from underneath it. What she was about to see now was much worse than what I had previously explained. Slowly, she removed the bandana from Jae's head. With every glance, I saw the pain on Dee's face. She cried when she saw Jae's head. But I did my best to encourage her by saying, "Come on now, Dee. We knew this was going to happen." I tried to show her the bright side. "Think about it, baby, if these hair cells are dying, that means the cancer is dying, too."

That day, we decided to let Jae take her first glance at her new look. After a quick, "Oh, nooo!" we distracted her with toys. She seemed disappointed that the hair she loved so much was gone. Day by day, a little more hair fell. But day by day, the uncomfortable feeling of seeing our daughter lose her hair subsided. I even shaved my head bald so that she would feel having a bald head was nothing less than normal. I did, however, worry about the possibility that she'd be stared at. Having no hair would tell everyone we came in contact with that she had some serious sickness. But by this time, I couldn't care less about what anyone else thought. She was beautiful, and her baldness represented the beginning of her healing to me.

We still hadn't made it public that Jae was battling cancer. But I decided it was at least time to let the world see her bald head. I took a picture and posted it to Facebook with the hashtag #JaeSTRONG. Social media erupted in praise over how beautifully bald she was. They didn't know exactly what she was going through. I'm assuming they knew something had to be wrong. However, my Facebook friends embraced her bald head and mine, too. We had noticed her first physical change. But what we would notice next, would be truly remarkable.

CHAPTER 14
Evidence of a Miracle Was in Progress

Almost every night, after we started this process, we'd gather in the master bedroom and do something fun together. Before Jae's diagnosis, it was normal for all of us to go our separate ways and enjoy individual time. But after all we had been through over the past couple of months, we clung to each other like we never had before, appreciating the precious moments we had together. Sometimes we'd play cards, watch movies, or just lay around talking about our day.

One of our favorite things to do was sing. Jae loved singing and especially liked this one song she had heard at church a few weeks earlier. This song became our theme song. The words of that song expressed precisely who we needed God to be. We'd sing the chorus regularly, not just because we liked the song, but because it meant so much to us. That chorus would ring throughout the house, "Way maker, miracle worker, promise keeper, light in the darkness. Our God that is who you are."

One night, while all of us were sitting in bed, Dee had Jae in her lap, getting her ready for bed. When she pulled off the shirt Jae had worn all day, Dee noticed the size of the cancerous tumor on her left shoulder blade had significantly decreased. Considering how large the growth was initially, this was a huge development. Though we were happy to see the swelling was decreasing right before our eyes, we had no way of knowing how significant of a development this was.

Upon our next visit to the hospital, Dee pointed out there was a visible decrease in the tumor size to Dr. Lagmay. When she took a look at Jae's shoulder, she, too, was amazed by what she saw. We witnessed the excitement all over her, and of course, we were ecstatic by her reactions. The doctor said something that let us know something major was happening. She said, "If the treatment produced this kind of result on her shoulder, it has to also mean that the tumors inside her body are shrinking."

She did, however, render a note of caution. She stated, "There's no way to be certain about what's really happening until I have an official scan," which Jae was scheduled to have after her fourth round of chemotherapy and just before the surgery. That would be months away, but that didn't dampen our spirits one bit. We were super excited and now had a way of determining how well she was progressing ourselves. We kept watching that shoulder, and day by day, we noticed the tumor shrinking. It was like we had front row seats to a miracle in progress.

Right before her third round of treatment, we noticed the tumor on her shoulder was completely gone. Yes, it was completely one. We were ready to get back to the hospital to show her doctor. If she had been that excited about how much the tumor had shrunk, surely, she would be amazed after seeing the tumor on her shoulder was gone. When we finally arrived at Shands for round three, we walked into the hospital feeling like prizefighters, who had won the last round. We were confident we were about to win this round in a big way. We couldn't wait for round three to begin. We were ready for them to examine her so that they could confirm what we already knew.

Most times, when the doctors walked into the room, they'd be professional, careful not to give us any false hope and moderate expectations. But on this day, Dr. Lagmay walked in with a team of doctors. They all seemed excited to examine her shoulder to see what had happened since the last time we were there. As Dr. Lagmay lifted Jae's shirt, we sat confidently as the other doctors inched closer for a better view. After her shirt was raised, I watched the amazement on all of their faces. There were audible gasps and exuberance in the room that's difficult to explain.

One young doctor pulled out his cellphone to snap pictures of this truly amazing site. Another doctor suggested Jae be sent in for scans before the appointment already scheduled so that they could get the proof of what they believed was happening. But Dr. Lagmay reigned in all the excitement. She was visibly pleased with what she saw. But she urged the young doctor with the camera not to take any photos; she didn't want any of us to get our hopes up too high over a one-dimensional image when a 3D image would tell the whole story.

Dr. Lagmay also rejected the suggestion that Jae be sent in for scans before the time previously scheduled. She suggested waiting until the fourth round of chemo was over. This didn't mean she didn't feel confident something amazing was happening; she wanted to maximize the effects of the current treatment plan without Jae having to go through any more scans than necessary. Though we were ready to know for sure the other tumors inside of her were shrinking like the one on her shoulder, we trusted Dr. Lagmay's judgment. We waited patiently. We'd go through the third and fourth rounds of chemo before we would know for sure. That day came on August 30, 2018.

The reason why some people will never understand how we can have #Joy in the middle of a storm ... is because what they see is a TRIAL ... but what we see is a TESTIMONY Brewing.

Unedited post to Facebook on June 25, 2018

CHAPTER 15

Grapes Taste So Much
Sweeter to Me Now

August 30, 2018 will forever be a day etched in my memory. I can recount everything about that day as if I experienced it yesterday. We had just completed two days of scans, and during those scan days, we had little communication with the doctors. A meeting had been scheduled the day after the last scans so that they could reveal the results to us. Dee seemed confident about the whole idea of waiting and receiving those results. If she had any anxiety, she didn't show any visible signs of being concerned. However, I was a nervous wreck and I had decided I didn't want to be present when the doctor came in to share the results.

Dee sat in the room, carelessly getting work done on her laptop, and Jae watched *Princess and the Frog* for the millionth time; I couldn't sit still. I spent much of the morning walking around the hospital, periodically peeking back into the room to see if Dee had heard anything. Jae's doctor had called early that morning saying she would be in to see us by eleven. But by 11 a.m., the doctor still hadn't arrived.

I was tired of pacing around the hospital and went back to the room to rest my feet. Considering her tardiness, I was certain the doctor would call before she came by. I was also certain Dee would alert me when she was on the way so that I could leave the room before she entered.

After drifting off to sleep, I slept without a care in the world. I'm not a heavy sleeper; I'm easily awakened by doors opening and conversations. That's how I woke up that afternoon around two o'clock. I was asleep on the pullout bed, and Dee was sitting in a chair not too far away. I heard the door open and heard Jae's doctor as she gleefully greeted Dee. Hearing all of the hustle and bustle woke me out of my sleep. Though I was awake, I didn't move an inch. I had been caught in the situation I had been dreading, being present when the doctor came in to reveal the results. My heart was racing, and anxiety was gripping me, but I still didn't move a muscle.

When the doctor started talking, she whispered, as if not to wake me. I could tell, even though she whispered, she was excited about whatever she was about to tell Dee. That's when the news broke. I overheard her saying the scans had shown something truly remarkable. Remember, I shared earlier this type of cancer could prove resistant to chemotherapy. The expectation was that as much as 50 percent of the tumors could remain after chemotherapy, which was the reason that surgery was so crucial. With a giggle in her voice, she told Dee that 90 percent of the cancer was gone, and the grapefruit-sized tumor in Jae's abdomen had shrunk to the size of a grape.

When she said that the grapefruit-sized tumor had shrunk to the size of a grape, I jumped out of my fake sleep and yelled, "A grape! Did you just say 90 percent is gone???"

Dee was praising God and I was now fully engaged, ready to hear the rest of the astonishing results. This revelation was especially significant, considering it would have been perfectly within the scope of expectation for four rounds of chemotherapy to only cause a grapefruit-sized tumor to shrink to a tennis ball-sized tumor. This was extraordinary news. God had begun a miracle that would shake the medical world and reshape the faith of the many who would hear our daughter's story.

Dr. Lagmay, who was as happy as we were about what had happened, elatedly confirmed the reports. As Dee and I hugged each other, she finished sharing the results. That's when it was revealed to me just how bad Jae's cancer was. She said, "The surgeon will be in tomorrow to explain his plan of action. Although 90 percent of the cancer is gone, there are still a few more spots that were found on the scans, including spots of cancer on her liver and pelvic. The surgeon will share the details of what the scans found and how he plans to operate when he meets with you all. But don't worry, this is great news!"

She hugged us and walked out of the room with this huge smile. Soon after she left the room, there was anything but a smile on my face. I felt deflated. Just thirty seconds earlier, I was the happiest I'd ever been in my life. But hearing that Jae had other spots in all these other places, made me sick to my stomach.

I looked at Dee and asked, "What does she mean other spots? Why is this good news if she still has cancer in so many other places?" I thought she just had the tumor in her abdomen. But that's when Dee reminded me of our, "You deal with the faith, and I'll deal with the facts," agreement. She said, "I knew all the time about how bad Jae's cancer was. I never told you because you couldn't handle knowing the extent of Jae's cancer." Now I wished I had known everything upfront. I went from being happy 90 percent of the cancer was gone to being disappointed that there were still cancerous spots clinging to my baby's body.

My mood pulled Dee's outlook down. All of the excitement in the room had left. We were staring into space, not looking forward to the meeting with the surgeon the next day. Anxiety had gripped me again; I renewed my intentions of not talking to any doctors about the results of those scans, and I didn't want to see the surgeon the next day. That meeting was scheduled for the early morning, so I did what I did the day before. I got up early and left the room. This time, I was determined to stay gone until Dee called me.

Waiting on her call was excruciating. I tried calling, but she never answered. Finally, while standing in line at the cafeteria, she called me back. Dee explained that she hadn't answered because the surgeon was in the room talking to her. I was trying to judge by the tone of her voice whether or not we'd gotten good or bad news. But I couldn't tell, so I just asked, "What did he say?" in an unenthusiastic manner.

She stated, "He basically said what Jae's primary doctor said yesterday." However, he added one key correction that changed everything. The surgeon, Dr. Islam, said that indeed the cancer in Jae's abdomen had shrunk from the size of a grapefruit to the size of a grape. But this doctor, who specialized in reading these scans, informed us that what the other doctor thought was grape-sized was more like a pebble-sized tumor. He added that though the tumor was small, it would still be an intricate surgery because of where it was located. The tumor was on her kidney and attached to her adrenal gland. He warned that surgeries like this could take up to eight hours and there was a risk of harm being done to her internal organs, especially her kidneys.

Dee explained the surgeon was positive he would be able to go in and get a substantial amount of the cancer. He also said, "If God is willing, I will be able to get it all." This was the first time a doctor or any medical professional had mentioned anything about God or invoked His will. Hearing this made me feel great. But there was one question I still needed to be answered, and until this point in the conversation, Dee hadn't mentioned it. So, I asked about all of the other tumors Dr. Lagmay had mentioned. What she said next caused me to shout so loud that the people standing in line with me at the cafeteria started staring at me like I had lost my mind.

Dr. Lagmay had told Dee to specifically ask the surgeon about the other spots she saw on the scans. Before she could get to her questions, the surgeon was preparing to leave the room as if the meeting was already over. But before he walked out, Dee asked. "Okay, you told me about the one tumor on her kidney, but what about the other tumors?" Dee said she was curious as to why he never mentioned the other spots in the first place.

He turned and asked, "What other cancer? All of the other cancer is gone!"

It turned out, he never mentioned the other spots, because what was originally thought to be cancerous spots, turned out to be nothing more than scar tissue left from cancer that was already dead.

I can't even begin describing the sheer joy that flooded my soul. God proved himself again as a miracle worker and a promise keeper. I'll always look at what I've seen occur in the life of our daughter as a necessary season that increased my faith in God. I never would have chosen any of this journey; I wouldn't wish what we've gone through on my worst enemy. Though I didn't choose this journey, knowing what I know now and seeing what I've seen, I wouldn't want to change it, either.

Overnight, I went from being disappointed over the news about Jae still having all these other cancerous spots to be being overjoyed that the good news was even better than we first thought, and the bad news should have never been news in the first place. At this point, we were ready for surgery. Yes, we knew how difficult surgery would be. Yes, we knew how much more pain our baby girl would have to endure. But we hung on to the last words the surgeon told Dee, "I don't believe that God has brought us this far not to finish the work." It was the day that I finally opened up about what we had been facing and shared our story with the world via Facebook.

CHAPTER 16
Tell the World

After hearing about the miracle on September 6, 2018, nearly three months after Jae was diagnosed with neuroblastoma, I finally decided to go public with what we had been facing. Until then, Dee and I had only shared what was going on with a few of our closest family and friends. People around us knew something medically was going on with Jae, but they had no clue about how serious the situation was. Dee had been ready to openly talk about our ordeal long before I was. She felt it was important for people who loved and cared about Jae, to know how to direct their prayers. Dee also wanted to put God on public trial. He had promised He was going to do it, so let us tell the world He said He was going to do it and watch Him prove Himself to be a God of His Word.

Before this date, I couldn't get the word cancer out of my mouth. There was even one instance, during a taping of my radio show, where Dee and I shared that Jae had been diagnosed with a serious illness. But I never said it was cancer. I asked for the prayers of my listening audience; I still couldn't bring myself to say we were in the fight of our lives against stage four, high risk, neuroblastoma. Instead, I told them, with a hint of glee, though the illness was serious, it was treatable, and we were confident everything was going to be fine.

At the end of that taping, Dee sat across from me in the studio, and asked, "Why couldn't you just be totally truthful about what was really going on? It's important to me that we not hide that this is a difficult time for us. Jae needs all the prayers she can get." She added, "I totally believe that God is going to heal Jae. I want the world to know how sick she is so that God will have extra incentive to heal my baby."

Publicly putting God's power on trial was her motive, and the result she was looking for was Him proving Himself mighty to people, who didn't believe, as well as solidifying the faith of those who did.

I understood everything Dee was saying, but I wasn't ready. I wasn't because I hadn't taken full ownership of our reality and couldn't admit that cancer was now a part of our reality. Talking specifically about cancer was too difficult for me. The thought of my baby girl having to fight cancer made me emotionally weak. I felt sorry for her. I felt sorry for me. I felt sorry for my family. I would eventually get past that feeling. Once I did, my reason for not wanting to tell anyone was because I didn't need anyone else feeling sorry for us. I sensed that once we opened up about Jae having cancer, our family would become the pit of everybody's pity, and Jae would become their symbol of sorrow. It was already tough enough to deal with what was going on, without the added burden of everyone else's concern. So, I mostly glossed over the details of our ordeal by projecting confidence that wasn't as solid as I was illuminating.

By the time I decided to reveal the news to the world that Jae had been diagnosed with cancer, she had already been through four rounds of chemo. It was after those four rounds of chemo that I fully understood the severity of what we were facing. Remember, I only knew that Jae had cancer because of the agreement Dee and I had made for me to only deal with the faith. I didn't have a clue there were tumors all over her body, nor did I know the cancer was already in stage four. It was after round four when we received the news that the grapefruit-sized tumor in her abdomen had shrunk to the size of a grape, and all of the other tumors had disappeared. That day was the day I knew I needed to share. My reason for opening up had less to do with the people's need to know about Jae's condition and more to do with a promise I had made to God when this journey began.

In our daily prayers, I always asked God to heal Jae. I always asked Him to heal her based on the condition that when He did, I would tell the world, so that he could get all of the glory. I didn't know exactly when that would be, but there was no doubt in my mind that one day, I would tell the story about what God had done. What we learned about Jae's cancer shrinkage was nothing short of miraculous. I couldn't hold it in any longer. I made a decision that day not to wait until the battle was over to glorify God.

After what I had heard, it was time. Even though we weren't through with the first phase of treatment, the miracles we were witnessing would not only glorify God but also give hope to every person hearing about what God was doing. We weren't out of the valley, yet a fire had been lit in my spirit. Jae's story could be an inspiration to others experiencing darkness if I only opened and shared the truth.

On September 6, 2018, with the support of Dee, I took to Facebook and wrote a long post that detailed everything we had experience from June 10th until that moment. Sharing the whole story and finally admitting to the world that my baby had cancer was made so much easier, considering I could end that post by sharing how Jae's cancer had miraculously shrunk. It took a few minutes before I got a response to the post, probably because it was a long read. Once reactions started coming in, they didn't stop. That post garnered over 5,500 likes, over 1,100 comments, and over 2,900 shares. Jae's journey had officially gone viral. From that day on, I chronicled every step of the journey.

Unedited post to Facebook on September 6, 2018:

On June 10ᵗʰ our lives took a shift that none of us were prepared for and presented my family with a test that would leave us at a breaking point. We were up early excitingly getting dressed for church when my wife noticed a large swelling on our daughter's left shoulder that seemed to come from nowhere. It definitely wasn't there the day before. Of course, we googled what it might be, but all of our searches were inconclusive, so we decided to take her to urgent care after church, knowing whatever it was couldn't be the worse we had seen online.

We took our baby to urgent care for what we thought would be a quick visit, but that quick visit slowly turned into a nightmare that lasted all day. From 1 PM until about 5 PM, doctors ran tests and ordered scans... each one coming back with results none of them knew how to decipher. Finally, around 5 PM a doctor walked in and ordered us to Tallahassee Memorial Hospital for further tests on more advanced equipment. His words said she would be fine. But his face said something is seriously wrong. We went from being hopeful that we'd figure out what it was to being scared to find out what it was.

We got to Tallahassee Memorial and test after test were conducted. Then around 10 PM that night, a doctor walked in rather nonchalantly and said ... "I believe your daughter has cancer. I'm sending you all to Shands for further evaluation." We were too shocked to cry ... too devastated to scream. The room was silent. Our baby was asleep peacefully after a long painful day, not knowing that her little life was hanging in the balance. I told the doctor that I would take her to Shands the next morning because all I wanted to do was get my family back to the safety of our home, if only for one night. But that doctor said in no uncertain terms ... "You can't go home, Sir. An ambulance will be here in an hour to transport her."

Finally, the reality had set in. Tears begin to fall, and they wouldn't stop falling at least for another four days. I went home as quick as I could and packed a bag for what I thought would be an overnight stay. I got back to the hospital and watched paramedics load my daughter on the ambulance. My wife rode along as I followed closely behind. When we got to Shands, we were quickly admitted, and more tests and scans were done. Around 5 AM on June 11th, the world as we knew it crashed. A doctor knelt beside a chair we were sleeping on. She whispered as not to awake the baby. She told us that the results of the scans are in, and "your daughter has a very aggressive form of cancer, and we need to start medications right way to stop the growth." I cannot tell you anything she said after that moment. Everything was dark and blurry. Her mouth was moving, but nothing was coming from her mouth.

Our baby had just been diagnosed with stage FOUR Cancer. I know exactly what kind it is, but I've purposely never called it by name because I disrespect it so much. She had a Grapefruit sized tumor in her abdomen that had spread to her kidney, liver, pelvic, and shoulder area. This was as bad as it gets. I told my wife early on that I didn't want to hear anything else the doctors had to say. She told me ... "I'll deal with the facts. You handle the faith." That became our strategy, and from that day, I never talked to any medical professional about my daughter's condition. I only talked to God.

Since June 11th, our daughter has been on a treatment plan. She's had FOUR grueling cycles of chemo, which have been accompanied by fevers and vomiting that have sent us back to the hospital several times. But though grueling, she's been a champion and doesn't look like what she's been through. She's amazed doctors at how the predictable side effects haven't affected her ... causing one doctor to say ... "If I didn't know she had cancer, I wouldn't even think she was sick." That meant a lot to us because we had been praying that God would allow our baby to go through this process without feeling the effects of the process. Our prayers and the prayers of others were working, and we had more faith than ever that we were going to get through this.

4 cycles into treatment, doctors scheduled a new set of scans to see how the cancer was responding to the chemo. We were warned not to expect more than 40 - 50 percent shrinkage. All that the chemo couldn't kill, prayerfully surgery would. We went into those scans apprehensive but believing God. For we had prayed every day and every night over that baby. We had people all around the WORLD praying for that baby. My Momma always reminded God of how much that baby loved him and worshipped him, begging him to give her another chance to come to church and worship ... but this time as a testimony. We wrapped her in a prayer handkerchief given to us by Gerald and Judy Mandrell every time she went to sleep. We knew what God COULD do. But the question remained ... would he do it?

On last week, we got the results of the new scans, and the news was nothing short of a miracle. Our main doctor walked in the room, laughing uncontrollably. She said the Tumor in our baby's abdomen had shrunk from the size of a Grapefruit to the Size of a GRAPE!!!! She said 90 percent is GONE!!!! I really didn't understand how significant that was until I found out that a normal treatment would only shrink a tumor from the size of a Grapefruit to a Tennis Ball. We were excited. But she warned that she still wanted us to talk to the surgeon because there were STILL spots on her liver, pelvic, and shoulder that was still there. We were excited about the news we had gotten. But, truthfully ... I dreaded meeting the surgeon because I knew there were so many other places the cancer still lived.

A day after the primary doctor came and shared the big news, my wife met with the surgeon alone. I had told her that I didn't want to talk to him. And the only thing I needed to hear was

that he could do the surgery successfully. He told my wife the
same thing as the doctor before him, about the Grapefruit sized
tumor in her abdomen that had miraculously shrunk. But this
doctor, who specializes in reading these scans, told her it's not
a grape-sized tumor, it's more like a little PEBBLE!!!! She had
been told by the previous doctor to ask questions about what
he planned to do about the other spots, but she was curious as
to why he never even mentioned the other spots. Turns out that
he never mentioned the other spots because the first doctor had
mistaken those spots for cancer when in actuality, those spots
were ONLY scar tissue that was left from cancer that was already
dead. He told my wife ... "All of the other Cancer is GONE!!!!

I shared this because there are so many people who doubt
God. But God is using our daughter to prove that he still reigns
supreme. He is truly a way maker, miracle worker, promise
keeper, light in the darkness. Surgery to remove that pebble is
scheduled for September 24th. But if God can shrink a Grapefruit
into a Pebble, SURELY, he can shrink a pebble into scar tissue.
That's what we are believing him to do. And even if he doesn't ...
in the words of the surgeon ... "I don't believe God has brought
us this for NOT to finish the work!" Believe God like you've
never believed God before. Because he's doing MIGHTY things
in the earth. I know ... because my baby is living proof.

From that day on, Jae's story became a beacon of hope to people
around the world. The way she gracefully fought this battle, smiling
all the way through, lifted the spirits of many people. And many
of those people reached out to us to share how Jae motivated them
daily, often mentioning that her strength had inspired them to fight
through their own battles. I didn't even know so many parents had
so many children battling cancer. But after we went public, they sent
messages to either encourage us or to tap into our faith. What we
were experiencing flowed over into their children's lives. There was
nowhere we could go without people coming up to us to share how

our journey was blessing them. I remember one instance; the mother of a child born with heart defects approached us in the mall. She said that her child wasn't given much of a chance to live. Because she had seen what God had done for Jae, her faith was ignited, and she believed God for her child's healing.

I can also recount another significant moment that occurred during one of our scheduled hospital stays. A young woman, who I had never met, had been keeping up with Jae's journey via Facebook. Ironically, she got diagnosed with the same kind of cancer as Jae. From viewing my page, she knew we were at the same hospital she had just been admitted to. She asked her nurse to find out where we were; she wanted to meet Jae face to face. She needed inspiration to fight a battle she never would've imagined she'd be facing when she started following our story. Due to Jae's weakened immune system, she wasn't allowed to visit that young lady. But I visited with her and was able to touch and agree with her for complete healing.

When I decided to go public, our fight wasn't over. We still had to face surgery, stem cell transplantation, radiation, and immunotherapy. We had at least another nine months to go in the process. But I was determined to share what we were experiencing, even if that meant I had to share our darkest moments during this journey. I felt that sharing the testimonies of all of the miracles we were witnessing was empowering people, and God was getting the glory that He so richly deserved.

"...Your life can go from flipped upside down to being flipped back to right side up in a matter of moments. Just hang in there long enough to see how God SHIFTS It. He's GONNA Do It!"

Unedited post to Facebook on October 1, 2018

CHAPTER 17
Come Get Me

The day of Jae's surgery was finally upon us. This was a critical stage in the process. What the surgeon saw when he opened her and what he was able to get out before he closed her, would determine the trajectory of our journey.

On September 24, four months and fourteen days after finding out Jae had cancer, we were at the hospital again. However, this time was different. Much was at stake. Our daughter was about to undergo a surgeon's scrapple, and her little body was about to be opened. That thought alone was tough on me. *That's my baby, and I'm about to release her into the hands of a surgeon that's about to cut her open.*

Those daunting thoughts slowly faded as I was reminded that she'd been in God's hands from the beginning of this process. God hadn't failed us yet, and I didn't believe He was going to fail us now.

As we sat in the waiting room for the process to begin, Dr. Islam came out, told us what his plans were, and what we should expect that early morning. It was around six in the morning, but he was bright-eyed. His conviction was so evident that any concerns I had were shattered by his faith in God and his surgical abilities. He explained that he had two choices regarding where he would make the incision. Based on where the tumor was, he'd rather make an incision down the middle of her stomach, which would be less painful for Jae during post-surgery. But he warned us that type of incision would lessen his access to the tumor. His other option was to make the incision through the muscle, just under her ribs, which would be more painful during post-surgery, but would increase his accessibility to the tumor. Honestly, it didn't matter to us. We trusted God, and we trusted him.

Dr. Islam reminded us of how long and difficult this surgery could hypothetically be due to the cancer's location, and that it was connected to her adrenal gland. He also warned us again about the potential harm that could be done to her kidneys and other vital organs. Dee was listening intently as she always did when the doctors talked, but I wasn't as focused. I was ready to get this over with. The final thing he shared was that his goal for this surgery was to remove as much of the tumor as he possibly could. He was adamant he would not take any unnecessary risks, trying to get all of this tumor. He preferred to leave her kidneys healthy and allow the chemotherapy to dissolve any disease he couldn't extract. He was basically saying that when the surgery was over and if he hadn't gotten all of the cancer out, he didn't want us to be alarmed. He assured us that he was going to get as much as he could get without damaging any of her other organs. Before leaving us for another conversation he had to have with his surgical assistant, he said, "If God is willing, I'll get it all."

We didn't have time to think about what he had said before his surgical assistant walked in and gave us the plan. She stated, "Once Jae goes back for surgery, I'll call to let y'all know what's happening step by step. I'll let y'all know when the anesthesia begins and when she falls asleep. I'll let y'all know when and where the incision is made. Also, I'm going to call y'all every hour to give an update on the surgery."

The last thing she told us was that once the surgery was over, the doctor would call to give us the results. My heart sank, not because I was nervous about the surgery. I trusted God, and I trusted the surgeon. But the thought of waiting until the doctor called, had my nerves in a tizzy. I was excited to get the show on the road, at the same time, waiting would be difficult.

Shortly after the surgeon's assistant left, a team of nurses came to take Jae away. She was asleep in her mother's arms, which was a good thing, because I dreaded the moment we would have to leave her in the hands of people she'd never known. Knowing she was asleep, meant I wouldn't have to hear her crying out for me like I knew she would have if she had been awake. As they walked off with her, one nurse cradling her as if she was a newborn, I wept. I walked off in front of Dee so that she wouldn't see that I was crying. When I composed myself, I grabbed her hands, and we prayed. This prayer was simple and had one central theme. We asked God to guide the surgeon's hands so that he might get all of this disease out of our baby's body. We walked off for breakfast in the cafeteria that neither of us ate.

While we were at breakfast, the surgical assistant called to inform us that Jae was being administered anesthesia. Before we headed back to the room, she called again, saying Jae was asleep and that the surgery was about to begin. Once in the room, she called to tell us the surgeon had made the incision, just beneath Jae's ribs, and that she would call us every hour until the surgery was complete. I was too nervous to stay in the room, so I left Dee to go outside for a walk. When I walked out of our room, I was met by Trevor Dunn, whose daughter had just been re-admitted to the hospital. Seeing his face and the conversation we had helped to take my mind off of waiting on these hourly calls. We stood in that hallway, outside our daughters' rooms, talking about everything from football to how grateful we were to have each other in our lives. I was in the middle of that conversation when my phone rang.

When I saw the phone number flashing across my screen, I thought it was the nurse calling to give us an update. A little over an hour had passed, so it was about time for her to call. As I stood right next to Trevor, I answered the phone. He stood by, respectfully, a short distance away so that I could talk to her. But the voice on the other end of the line wasn't that of the surgical assistant; it was

Dr. Islam. This was quite confusing because I wasn't expecting his call until the surgery was over, and the surgery was supposed to last hours, potentially eight hours. My heart raced. I didn't have a clue about why he'd be calling after only an hour. *What could have possibly gone wrong?*

His exact words were, "Mr. Jackson, I just called to let you know that the surgery is over, and it was a success. I got all the cancer …" he continued talking. Only I had dropped my phone from my ear, and it was dangling somewhere around my knees. My body went limp. When I placed the phone to my ear again, the only other thing I heard him say was that Jae was headed to recovery, and we should be able to see her shortly. I profusely expressed my thanks to him, to which he replied, "God was gracious."

Trevor had been listening from a short distance away. When he realized the news that I had gotten had to be amazing, he rushed over and grabbed me up in a bear hug. He held me like we had just won a Super Bowl together. While crying in his arms, I said, "They got it all, man. They got it all." My head was on his shoulders, and his head was in mine. We wept in sincere thanks for what God had done. This moment was not just special for me, though, it was also especially significant for Trevor.

A few weeks earlier, his daughter had gone through the same surgery, but the news he had gotten wasn't as favorable as the news I'd just received. Even after surgery, his daughter still had a significant amount of cancer left in her body. So much cancer was left that they'd have to endure an extra round of treatment, trying to get it all. Yet, he celebrated with me as if the victory we had just won was his own. Honestly, it was his victory, too. He told me how happy he was about what God had done for Jae because this was all the proof he needed that God was about to work a miracle in his daughter's life, too, and that a miracle for Brooke would soon follow. Releasing his hold on me, Trevor said, "You better get in that room and tell Dee the great news! So, I hurriedly heeded that advice.

When I walked into the room, she was sitting on the bed calmly, playing some game on her phone. I said, "The doctor called," trying to temper my voice so that I could maximize the impact of the news I was about to share.

She replied, without even glancing up, "Okay, what did they say?" She undoubtedly thought I was about to give her the first update. I can't blame her for that thought process, because we had been prepared to get several updates over a span of hours. Surely, I couldn't have possibly been coming into the room to say what I was about to say. I tried to make breaking the news to her as dramatic as possible, but I couldn't hold it in any longer. I just blurted it out, "They got it all!"

"They got all what?" she asked, building her excitement level.

"The surgery is over, and he got ALL of the cancer!" You can't begin to imagine the euphoria in that room. We both were overwhelmed with joy. We embraced. We cried together, and we celebrated before calling all of our family to share this amazing news.

Two days later, Jae was recovering faster than expected. We had been advised to expect her to start trying to walk after four days. But after only two days, this strong little girl had already bounced back. Dr. Islam walked in that day to check on her and told us what we were witnessing was nothing short of a miracle. He said that when he opened Jae for surgery, it was as if the tumor had already released itself form everything it was connected to and was calling out to him, "Come get me."

Dr. Lagmay walked in a little later during the day and shared that Dr. Islam had been telling Jae's story all over the hospital. Dr. Lagmay never really mentioned faith in our conversations with her. Though she was incredibly encouraging with her tender words and heartfelt hugs and smiles, faith was just something she never revealed through conversation. But on this day, Dee forced her to admit what she was witnessing. Her words to us that day were, "This is unprecedented! Unheard of! Chemo alone didn't do this." Dee replied, "It was God; a miracle." to which Dr. Lagmay smiled and nodded in affirmation.

Your Trial is only God's TOUCH away from being a Testimony about your Triumph.
- Clarence Jackson

CHAPTER 18
The Storm is Almost Over

On October 8, Jae began her final round of chemo. The last round of chemo was by far the hardest one. Jae vomited more violently and was sicker than I had ever seen her. This wasn't the hardest round because of how taxing these days were on her body; nausea and vomiting paled in comparison to the truth that on the day we checked in for the last round of chemo, a Category 4 hurricane was barreling directly toward our hometown. Due to Dee's role as county administrator, she was unable to travel with us to Gainesville. Because of how devastating Hurricane Michael became, she was unable to join us at all for the final. I had been alone with Jae several days, just as Dee had when I had to work, but this time was different. The chemo was taking its toll on Jae, and the hurricane was taking its toll on my family back home. The combination of those two things was taking a toll on me. It felt like Jae and I were alone for the first time through all of this.

Most times, if I felt uncomfortable about what was happening with Jae, I'd find comfort in calling Dee or my sister or my mother. Early on in our stay, I lost total communication with all of them because the hurricane not only took out power, it also took out cellphone service. Thus far, Jae had won every round of chemo quite easily, but this last round was brutal. It was like she was taking vicious body blows and head shots, and there was nothing I could do to protect her from any of these happenings. I didn't have the comfort of having Dee to share the load, and Jae didn't have her mother to soothe her pain as only a mother could.

One night, I wanted to take a picture of Jae to see if she would give me her trademark smile. When I pointed the camera at her, her brows were stuck in a frown; illustrating how much pain she was experiencing. It's probably the most memorable photo I took of her during this whole journey. It showed her pain. Yet, with only a few more chemo treatments left, it showed her will to win. Though she wasn't smiling, she looked directly into that camera with a scowl, as if to say, "Daddy, I may be tired and hurting, but I'm not giving up." And she didn't give up. She fought like hell every day. Though we were alone, without any communicating with the people we loved, we had each other.

By the last day of chemo, the hurricane was over, but our county had been ravaged. I had seen some of the devastations on the news and was concerned about what had happened to our home and family. That concern peaked when I heard on CNN there was at least one confirmed death due to the storm and possibly more, just miles from where my family lived. My anxiety escalated when one of the doctors came in and said that due to the catastrophic events surrounding the hurricane and power outages in our county, he wouldn't be releasing Jae. It was too dangerous of a situation to put her in, considering some of the medicine she would need required refrigeration. I understood his concerns, but I needed to be close to my family. I wanted to know if they were okay. I also wanted to get out of that hospital room. This had been the toughest week of our journey, and with power out indefinitely, there was no end in sight.

I finally started hearing from home, and all of my family was safe. Our home only suffered a little damage. Outside of the tall pine tree that fell inches away from our house, all was well. This was, in some ways, a metaphor of what we'd experienced since June 10th. We had experienced a major storm. Although we had seen damages, we were alive, and everything the storm destroyed, we were able to rebuild. We lived through it and had an opportunity to fight another day.

The only thing that gave me a slither of peace and happiness that week was the second that last bit of chemo dripped from the little clear bag into her veins. Whenever any medicine finished running, there would be a beeping sound alerting the nurses that the round was over. I was waiting, sitting on the edge of the bed that night, waiting on that sound as if it was the bell signaling the end of the last round of a prizefight we had marched her into months earlier. She had been battered and bruised. If she could hang on just a little while longer, she would have won another round and this fight.

When the machine began beeping, I wept in sheer joy. She had done it. She had successfully gone through five rounds of chemo and surgery. That was significant because when she started this fight, she had tumors all over her body, and in her bones, one the size of a grapefruit on her kidney. By the time she finished, all of the visible signs of cancer were gone. That night, I lifted her above my head and said, "You did it Baby. I'm so proud of how you fought." Though she was drained, she managed to smile at me. She had won.

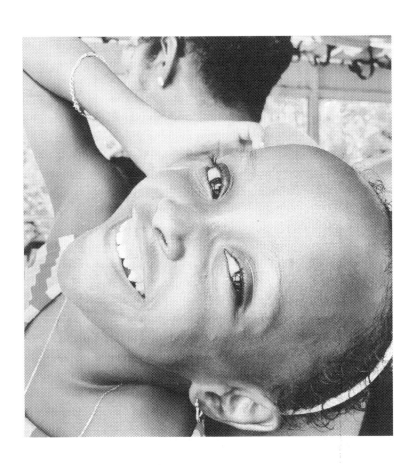

CHAPTER 19
Jae is a Producer

U nlike many children, who suffer from the same kind of cancer Jae had, she would go into stem cell transplantation completely cancer-free. As comforting as that was, the stem cell transplantation had the potential to be just as grueling of a process as chemotherapy. If, for no other reason, the transplantation would be tough because this would be the part of the process to test our endurance the most. We had already been warned this process could take up to forty-five days, and Jae would have to be hospitalized for the duration of that time. After the transplantation, we would have to stay no further than thirty minutes from the hospital for another extended period.

We had already spent more time in hospital rooms than we had in our living room since the day she was diagnosed. The prospect of being away from home for such a long time was an intimidating thought. All the potential adverse effects of this phase of the journey wore on our psyche as well. Jae had been remarkably strong during chemo; now, we were faced with a challenge we hadn't seen.

Before I get into the details about key moments during the process, I need to explain why this step was so necessary for Jae. She had been through five rounds of harsh chemo, which destroyed her stem cells. Therefore, she needed a procedure that would reintroduce healthy blood-forming cells into her body to replace the ones destroyed by the disease or the high doses of anticancer drugs she had received. The healthy stem cells she would receive would come from her if she was able to produce enough. If she couldn't produce enough of them, she would have to receive some from a donor, which would increase the likelihood of her rejecting those stem cells. We had to go through a process before the actual transplantation to see if she could produce enough healthy stem cells. We were grateful there were options in case she couldn't; our prayer was that she'd be full of healthy stem cells that she could later receive when the time warranted.

What I remember most about the day Jae was tested for healthy stem cells was that it was a much more relaxed process than I'd anticipated. It was as simple as them connecting her to this machine that extracted the stem cells and waiting for results from the lab. They said Jae needed to be able to produce at least 13 million healthy cells; I couldn't see how even one hundred healthy stem cells could fit in the little bag hanging from the machine, collecting them. Nevertheless, my focus wasn't on the miracle of medical technology as much as it was on the results of this procedure. What happened on this day would significantly increase or decrease our chances of a successful transplantation.

We waited all day long for results from the lab. Finally, Dr. Horne, a world-renowned stem cell specialist, walked in and told us how amazing what had just happened was. Her exact words were, "I've never seen anything like this. Her stem cells were jumping all over the place."

The results showed that Jae not only produced the 13 million healthy stem cells needed to ensure she wouldn't need a donor, but Jae had also produced 78 million of them. This meant she had produced enough healthy stem cells for her to become someone else's donor one day. Somebody, somewhere in the world, would get a second chance at life because our baby girl produced this day. Later, we learned Jae had produced enough healthy stem cells to be a blessing to at least five people.

Knowing what we knew now, made going into the transplantation phase a little easier to deal with. But there was still a huge elephant in the room that Dee and I never wanted to talk about. How in the world are either of us going to be able to spend so much time away from our responsibilities, especially when every medical professional we talked to was saying that both of us needed to be by Jae's side because of all the things expected to happen.

Dr. Kissoon, a young energetic doctor who was always brutally honest in the most serious manner she knew how, said, "This is going to be really tough, and one parent isn't going to be able to handle this alone."

She described all of the possible side effects, including potential seizures. Also, she told us soaring fevers were going to occur. She painted a grim picture, and it mirrored what we had heard from other parents of children who had gone through this process, and other doctors and nurses alike. Only we had seen God do so many miraculous things through Jae, and He had proven Himself able to significantly decrease the occurrences of side effects time after time. There wasn't any doubt in our minds that God would do it again. As she knelt beside us, saying what we should be expecting, our expectation was already sealed, and ours was the polar opposite of hers.

Patiently, we waited for her to finish speaking. When she was done and asked if we understood everything, Dee responded, "None of that is going to happen to Jae."

Going into the transplantation, we didn't have any plans. We didn't know how long either of us would be able to stay with Jae or if there would ever be a time both of us could stay during the process. What we knew was that God had done exceedingly, abundantly, above all that we had asked or thought so far. We had no reason to doubt that this stage of the journey was going to be any different. I will admit, I had dreaded the day this long process would commence. But now, I was ready. I even made this bold prediction on my Monday radio show: "This process won't last forty-five days. We will be back home in under thirty days."

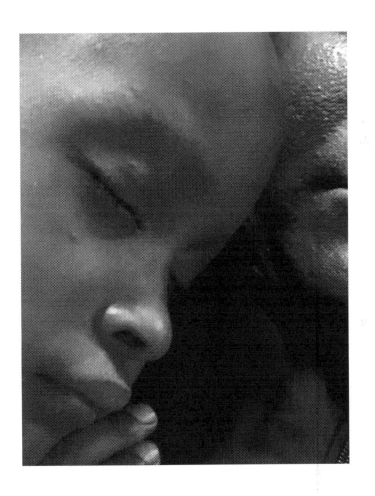

CHAPTER 20
The Rise Begins

O n November 5, Jae's stem cell transplantation began. This process took more endurance than I had ever had to exhibit. During this long stay in the hospital, I saw God clearer than I had ever seen Him. I was in my wilderness moment. I consistently spoke to Him, and He clearly spoke to me. I talked to him a lot because I needed Him so much during this time. I'm also thankful He clearly talked to me. I needed to hear everything He had to say. It wasn't as if this stage in the process was more difficult than any other we had faced, but the duration started to take its toll on me after a while. Even on the darkest days, I saw God, and He spoke to me.

The process began quite uneventfully. The first week included Jae having to be injected with the strongest dose of chemo she had received thus far. The purpose of such a strong dosage was so that she would be completely drained of all of her remaining bone marrow. Because of this strong round of chemo, it was expected that Jae would experience nausea and vomiting and develop mucositis, which was a painful inflammation and ulceration of the mucous membranes lining the digestive tract. They said Jae would have severe pain from her mouth, through her digestive tract, down to her bottom. Due to the predicted severe pain, she was injected in advance and throughout the process with a steady flow of morphine to help ease her agony. They said that at some point, she would stop eating and drinking because swallowing anything would feel like swallowing sandpaper. We were also warned that Jae could develop liver disease during this process. Extra pillows were placed all around her bed due to the probability of having seizures. As week one progressed, we saw little change in her condition or disposition.

Doctors and nurses said that this would probably be the worst week of the transplantation process, and we should expect to see a weakened little girl. But Jae went through four days of this extra strong chemo treatment without any nausea or vomiting, no seizures, and no fevers. She didn't show any signs that she was in any pain. By day five, the chemo portion of the transplantation was over. To all of her doctors' surprise, Jae had waltzed through it, proving once again that God's hands were clearly on her, and He was blessing us according to our expectations. On day six, I wrote this Facebook post to celebrate what God had done.

> #Day6: Today, we had to settle for a FaceTime conversation. I came home for church. But I can't wait to get back to my girls. Chemo is DONE! Today through Monday are rest days ... and then Tuesday is the BIG Day. That's the day her body will be reintroduced to her own healthy cells. That's when her little body will be put through a major test. But we are confident in her strength. We've seen too much of it to be afraid now. Thank God for 6 uneventful days. We are believing God that the 30-45 Days we've planned to be here will be cut down to under 30. Believe with us. #JaeStrong

After the successful extraction of all of her old stem cells via the chemo treatment, Jae had her actual stem cell transplantation on November 13th. This was a special day for us because stem cell transplantation day is also called the day of rebirth. Patients who went through this process normally considered this day a second birthday. Some of our family and friends even visited bearing gifts with the inscription "Happy Birthday." I had gone into this day, thinking it was going to be something hugely out of the ordinary. But much like the day they extracted her stem cells, this day was fairly uneventful.

The nurse came in with a little syringe, filled with 13 million healthy stem cells she had extracted earlier. For twenty minutes or so, they slowly injected them into Jae's bloodstream. Just like that, it was done. All that was left was for us to see how her body responded to her new stem cells. At the start, nothing much seemed to change. Outside of a little nausea and being irritable, nothing major happened. She was sailing through this process so far, and just like Dee had predicted, our baby girl wasn't experiencing anything that the medical professionals had told us to expect, not even the slightest fever. By day eleven, things began to change. I posted this on Facebook to explain what I felt when the tide started shifting.

#Day11: Typically, I post HIGHlights of our days here at Shands. But there are LOWlights as well. Although 80% of this visit has been praiseworthy ... the other 20% requires a lot of strength from Jae and a lot of STAMINA from those of us caring for her. Last night was one of those moments. She woke up around 1 AM vomiting due to mucositis, which is pretty common during stem cell transplant. Several times during the early morning, she'd have an episode. I'm certain it's uncomfortable for her to endure, and it's definitely uncomfortable to watch. She wouldn't go back to sleep the rest of the morning, but I'm totally fine with that because I know that every night that we go through episodes like this is one step closer to this process being complete.

Due to the onset of mucositis, which was going to get worse before it got better, Jae hadn't eaten or drank anything. The doctors paid careful attention to her loss of appetite and ordered a nutritional supplement to ensure she wouldn't become dehydrated or lose more energy than she could afford while she wasn't eating. On day thirteen, she surprised all of us when she asked for something to eat. I understood that swallowing anything would feel like she was swallowing sandpaper, but this girl reached out and begged for some of the potato chips I was eating. She didn't eat many; still, this was a clear sign her body was healing more rapidly than the doctors had predicted.

On day fourteen, Jae started mounting her comeback from the chemo treatment and showing signs that the stem cell transplantation was producing results. What I hadn't explained before now was that the strong dosage of chemo was designed to bring her Absolute Neutrophil Count (ANC) down to zero. A zero, at any other moment during this process, would have meant disaster. But a zero on day fourteen meant sweet success. Jae had hit what he termed, "Rock Bottom," which was the exact place her doctors needed her to be. Having him tell us that her ANC was at zero was as big of a celebration as when we learned Jae had produced 78 million healthy cells. Being at zero meant the tide had turned in our favor; it also meant she was susceptible to fevers until her ANC fully recovered.

By day eighteen, Jae still didn't have any fevers. Despite all of the warnings about her becoming a weak little girl, though she wasn't eating and drinking as much as the doctors wanted her to eat or drink, Jae was anything but weak. She wasn't even showing any signs of pain. Because she wasn't showing any signs of discomfort, the doctors decided to start weaning her off of the morphine. They said that as her ANC increased, her body would begin to heal quickly from the painful effects of the mucositis. We waited every evening for the night shift nurse to come in around ten to tell us Jae's numbers. Every uptick in her ANC would mean she was healing quickly.

Jae had been at zero for a couple of days. Though we celebrated zero on day fourteen, we were about sick of it after that number didn't rise as quickly as we wanted it to. We needed to see something other than that to prove this stem cell transplantation was going as planned. We had been advised that seeing movement in her numbers would take a few days, but I was growing impatient. I waited up every night for that nurse to give us some good news. Yet, night after night, she told us that Jae was still at zero.

On day nineteen, the nurse walked in with a smile and said, "We got some movement. It's a small number. But after tonight, we expect to see her numbers rise quickly." I was ecstatic. Although that number was only 0.5, I was excited because it was higher than zero. We had been in the valley for a few days, but that 0.5 meant we were headed to the mountaintop and could be headed home sooner than anyone expected.

After hearing the news that Jae's ANC had risen and knowing any rise in her numbers would mean we would see dramatic increases each day, we excitedly anticipated the nurse coming in every night. Jae had to reach 500 before she would be considered for release. Not only did she have to reach 500, but Jae would also have to maintain it for at least three days.

On day twenty, the nurse walked in with another update. I shared what we learned on Facebook, so our family and friends would know that God was hearing and answering all of our prayers.

#Day20: On yesterday, we chose to praise God for an ANC of 0.5... knowing full well that Jae needed at least a 500 to be considered for release. Our #Praise was strategic. Though we knew we weren't where we needed to be, we chose not to despise SMALL Beginnings. We believed that if we praised God for a "little" he would bless us with a "lot." Well ... this morning, Jae's ANC has jumped from 0.5 to 757!!!!! If she maintains an ANC of 500 or better for 3 Days, she will be ready for #RELEASE barring any unforeseen setbacks. We asked you all to pray and believe with us that this process wouldn't last the 30-45 days predicted. Now we're asking on day 20 that you pray and believe God with us that there will be NO SETBACKS between now and Tuesday. #Jae757 #JaeStrong

CHAPTER 21
Here Come the Setbacks

O nce Jae crossed that 500 threshold, it was no looking back. The day after we got the news her ANC had jumped from 0.5 to 757, we received the news that her ANC had risen again and was now at 1449! What we were witnessing was unbelievable. We would be going home in a few days; well under the thirty days I had predicted. But there was one problem. Jae hadn't suffered any fevers; she hadn't experienced any seizures, and she hadn't developed that dreaded liver disease that would have landed her in the intensive care unit (ICU). The only thing she suffered was the mucositis; we were told it would go away once her numbers started to rise.

We were confident the mucositis had subsided because Jae still didn't show any signs of pain after they started weaning her off of the morphine. But even though she shouldn't have any problems swallowing, she still wasn't eating like she needed. Her doctors were ready to take her off of the nutritional supplement, but there was no way they would consider that unless she started eating on her own. Ready to go home and knowing all that was keeping us from going home was Jae's eating, I sent out a prayer request for all of our family and friends to pray that she regained her appetite. I asked one doctor, "Why would Jae not be eating if she's not in any pain?"

Her answer gave me a revelation I'll carry with me for the rest of my life and share with as many people that will listen. She replied, "Jae is not eating, not because she's in any pain. She's not eating because of the memory of the pain she had the last time she swallowed."

On day twenty-one, I'd share this revelation with my family and friends on Facebook. I prayed that what God showed me blessed them. Here's what I wrote:

God just showed me something very powerful through Jae's deliberate refusal of food and drink. She's not eating and drinking, NOT because she's in any pain. The pain left days ago. She's not eating and drinking because of the MEMORY of her pain. She survived the worst part of the process ... yet her MEMORY is preventing her from getting her release. How many of you have survived the worst parts of your life ... yet you're not living free because you're paralyzed by the MEMORY of what happened to you? You'll never "Live Your Best Life" if you continue to let the memory of what you've been through, be the prominent thought in your mind.
Here's your word ... It's Over! You Survived It! LIVE!

Though I now had a better understanding of why Jae wasn't eating, it still didn't stop me from being frustrated over the fact that she wasn't eating. By day twenty-one, I was more frustrated. I was with Jae by myself during this time. I did everything in my power to try to get her to eat. I'd even put applesauce in a syringe and try to force it down her throat to prove to her that she wasn't going to be in any pain if she swallowed.

Every attempt I made was met with her nonchalantly spitting it back out as if she could care less about going home. All she was doing was sitting around all day listening to "Baby Shark," as I tried unsuccessfully to get her to eat. I was ready to go home. I was frustrated that this one simple thing was keeping me from going home. I even caught myself yelling at her, "Come on, man! Eat!" I'm sure some people are chastising me right now, but unless they have been in this position, they wouldn't know this feeling. But the way God Chastised me on day twenty-two was greater than any rebuke anyone could ever give me. Oh, yea, God rebuked my frustration, and I shared this chastisement via Facebook.

#Day 22... "here you are at the end of this journey, and you're frustrated because you don't know when you're going to get there, and you have no control over how you're going to get there. You haven't been in control this whole time. But now that you're at the end ... you wanna rush the process? I've been taking care of this baby since day one. Healed her from stage four cancer, and now you want to question me ... at the end? Instead of counting how many steps you got left to the finish line, why don't you start counting the miles you are from where you started from?"

That rebuke changed my whole outlook. I was no longer in a rush to get home. I even threw my "under thirty days" prediction out of my mind. My focus now was on the fact that her doctors were blown away by how she had sailed through the process. My focus now was that the little girl that I was just upset with for not eating was sitting in her bed without having any fevers, seizures, or liver disease. I stopped being focused on when this process would end and started focusing on the fact it was already coming to an end.

On day twenty-five, Jae still wasn't eating. But I wasn't frustrated anymore. I considered these remaining days, no matter how many more they were, as our victory lap together. The doctors had deemed this a successful transplantation. As soon as she ate, we could head home.

I wasn't stressing, and the doctors didn't seem to be, either. On this day, they disconnected her from every medicine and nutritional supplement she had been taking. Their theory was that if she didn't have the nutritional supplement, maybe her hunger would be stimulated, and she would be more inclined to eat. Despite that strategy, she still wouldn't eat or drink, and her sugar levels dropped dangerously low. The doctor didn't hesitate to put her back on the nutritional supplement because low sugar levels were too dangerous of a proposition.

On day twenty-seven, I noticed her doctors were getting a bit concerned. Just after I left to return home for church, they informed Dee that they believed Jae's body was going into starvation mode. This meant she had gone so long without food that her body had stopped recognizing its need for food.

Dee called me and said the only option they had was to proceed with a plan they had discussed to insert a feeding tube in hopes of stimulating her stomach. Hearing this broke my heart. Dee heard the hurt in my voice. She tried to ease my hurt by saying, "The doctors said that although Jae needs a feeding tube, it wouldn't have to stay in long. They're even willing to send her home with the feeding tube until she develops a more substantial appetite." Dee seemed fine with that idea. But for me, the thought of a feeding tube started to spoil what had otherwise been a successful process. I hated I wasn't going to be there for my baby when they did this. At the same time, I was happy I was gone because I knew I wouldn't be able to handle watching them slide a tube through her nose into her stomach as she screamed.

Though I hated the idea of my baby needing a feeding tube, I didn't question the doctors' plans. God had directed them, and we had seen supernatural results. There wasn't a question in our minds about whether or not to agree to it.

Once Dee gave them the okay, a few minutes later, a couple of nurses walked into the room to begin the procedure. Dee said she painfully watched as those nurses forced this tube through Jae's nose and down into her stomach, all while she was wide awake. Dee said Jae screamed and fought like she was in a battle for her life, scratching, and clawing at those nurses as if her will could overpower theirs. Even if her will couldn't overpower theirs, Jae had made inserting that tube a more difficult process than it would have been had she relaxed.

Regardless of her greatest efforts to resist their efforts, the nurses won; they were finally able to get the tube in. However, after they secured the tube and were satisfied with its placement, Jae did the unthinkable. Without any warning or hesitation, Jae grabbed that feeding tube and snatched it out of her nose. Seeing what happened, the nurses came up with a plan to go with another type of tube, which would go a little deeper than the one Jae pulled out. So, they left the room to retrieve the longer feeding tube.

As they were exiting the room, Bethany, an always sweet, child life specialist, who had always been great with handling Jae when she was experiencing anxious or painful moments, walked into the room. She had heard all of the commotions in Jae's room and came in to see if she could calm Jae down. What happened next was truly amazing. In between the time the nurses left to get the new tube and returned, Bethany told Jae that if she ate, she would give Jae a sticker. And just like that, to everyone's surprise, Jae took a bite. With every challenge and promise of reward from this sweet lady, Jae took another bite. Dee said that before those nurses walked back into the room, Jae was not only eating, but she had also taken another bribe and started drinking, too. Instantaneously, we had gone from the prospects of having a feeding tube inserted down her nose and into her stomach to a point where she was eating and drinking on her own. From that moment, Jae ate and drank consistently, and her sugar level rose significantly. I learned something valuable through all of this, and I shared the revelation on my Facebook page on December 1, 2018:

Here's the powerful lesson I got out of all of this. The doctors wanted to insert a feeding tube. But Jae FOUGHT IT. Even though they overpowered her and forced it in ... Jae snatched it out. See ... there are times when things you don't want will be forced upon you. But if you Fight ... you can Resist and Reject what you know isn't ordained by God for your life. As soon as Jae snatched out that feeding tube ... her appetite came back. God is saying to YOU... as soon as you Resist and Reject what the enemy is trying to do in your life, you'll begin to see the hand of God move in ways you never thought were possible.

With her appetite now reenergized, her sugar levels finally stabilized. Due to how well she was progressing behind an unforeseen turnaround, doctors disconnected her from the nutritional supplement again. They said that they were going to monitor her sugar level throughout the night and all the next day. If her sugar level remained stable, they would send us home.

On December 3rd, twenty-nine days following the first stem cell transplantation, Jae was cleared for release. The prediction I had made of "under thirty days" had turned into prophecy.

CHAPTER 22
Delayed but Not Denied

F resh off of a successful stem cell transplantation, we were geared up for the next phase, which was radiation. We already knew this could be another long process that potentially involved many days away from home. A series of scans showing the radiologists if and where there was any disease left would determine how many days we would have to do radiation. We had been through this kind of scan before. The first time Jae had scans like this, Dee said that she remembered seeing these bright colors popping up on the screen from where she was sitting. Those bright colors were evidence of every place Jae had cancer, basically all over her body. Knowing what we knew about how Jae's cancer had dissolved after chemo and was completely gone after surgery, we went into those scans much more confident than the last time.

Only one of us was able to accompany Jae. There was no question that Dee would be the one to go in. She had done this before and knew exactly what she was looking for. When they were escorted back into the room, I took my traditional walk around the hospital and waited on the news. The scans only took about thirty minutes or so, but it took a couple of days for results to be reviewed by doctors, who would then present them to us.

When Dee called to tell me the scans were done, I sensed in her voice that something good had happened. She said, "As I was watching the screen, I didn't notice any of the bright colors that had flashed across the screen the first time Jae had these scans done and was full of cancer. I asked one of the technicians in the room if what I didn't see was any indication that there was no cancer present."

The technician wouldn't give a definitive answer, deferring to the expert's opinion that would be shared a few days later. But the technician said that what Dee was thinking wasn't far from the truth.

We waited two days for the results, but we were ready this time. When we received them, they were just as we expected. The scans showed no signs of cancer. Instead of the twenty-one days or more that we were looking at when we got started, they said that Jae would only have to go through eight days of low dosage radiation. Because of the low dosage, side effects weren't that big of a concern for her doctors. We felt elated as if Jae would breeze through this process. We were also relieved, considering how we had gone from trying to figure out living arrangements in Gainesville for at least twenty-one days to now considering whether or not we could make that two-and-a-half-hour drive to the hospital every day for eight days. Before we would go too far trying to answer that question, I had another question that was a bit puzzling.

The question I had was if the scans didn't show any signs of cancer, why did Jae need radiation? The answer to that question gave me another revelation. One doctor explained that though Jae was technically cancer-free, it was important to treat the cancer bed, the area in her abdomen, where most of the cancer was and the area on her shoulder, where the cancer first visibly manifested.

When I heard this, God began speaking to me. He said that there were times when we were delivered from people, places, and things. But to break toxic cycles and ensure that there were no reverberating effects of what we encountered, we had to make sure every area those people, places, and things affected were completely healed. Jae didn't need radiation because she had cancer; she needed radiation because the cancer had left a trail the doctors never wanted that cancer to travel again. God said, "It's one thing to have fixed what was wrong. But to have lasting effects, you must also fix where it came from, which is the root of the issue."

On January 8, 2019, Dee and I woke up at three in the morning, left the house at four, and drove Jae to Gainesville to be on time for her seven o'clock appointment for radiation. Something happened when we got there that frustrated me. Though we had planned for eight days of radiation, we were informed upon our arrival that Jae was scheduled for twelve days. That startling bit of news threw us for a loop.

After repeating what we thought were the doctor's orders, one of the nurses called Jae's doctor to see where the confusion might be. It turned out, the radiologist had recommended eight days, but after initially agreeing to that duration, Dr. Lagmay opted for Jae to have the twelve days minimum standard of care.

I got to admit that I was fuming. This new development had thrown a monkey wrench in all of our plans. I was quickly calmed by the understanding that whether it was eight or twelve days, the process was about to begin. Completing this stage in the process had encountered a slight delay. An additional four days wasn't about to destroy my view of the successful long road we had already traveled. Our blessing may have been delayed, but it had not been denied.

After clarifying all of the confusion about how many days Jae would have to go through radiation, it was now time for the process to begin. Once the machine was warmed and ready and the anesthesiologist arrived, Jae and I were ushered back to the room. This procedure required that Jae be put to sleep every day to ensure this targeted approach to treatment wouldn't be less successful because she moved. Moving an inch could have been dangerous. When we got into the room, I sat on the bed, holding Jae in my arms.

The anesthesiologist administered a small dose of medicine, and in minutes, she drifted off to sleep.

Once she was asleep, I placed her into a little mold made especially for her and walked out. When I turned that first corner, I paused for a moment and cried. After shedding a few tears, I wiped my eyes and went to the waiting room to wait with Dee until the twenty-minute process was done. About thirty minutes later, they rolled Jae out for what would be a thirty-minute stay in recovery to carefully watch every move until she woke up. By eight, the process was over. We were on our way back home to get ready to do it all again the next day.

Sometimes we make plans ... based on our limited knowledge. And God allows us to make those plans because He gives us free Will. But when what we plan ... doesn't match what HE Planned ... He Loves us enough to Change those plans in a way that HE knows is best for us. So, when things seem like they are taking a little longer than planned. Don't be so quick to get angry about how long what you're looking for lingers. Keep in mind that God is always in Control ... and that delay you've been complaining about ... might just be God saying you need more time in it ... so that you'll never have to go back through it.

Unedited post to Facebook on January 10, 2019

CHAPTER 23
Dark Lonely Road

T welve days of radiation was quite uneventful. Every day was a repeat of the previous day. We'd walk into the room, they'd put Jae to sleep, approximately twenty minutes later, they'd roll her up to recovery, and she'd wake up within thirty minutes. After she showed proof that she could drink something and hold it down, we would be released. I always packed two or three Capri Suns in her bag because those were her favorite drinks. She woke up every morning after a radiation session and asked for her "orange juice." There were a few times, on the way back home, that I had to pull over to the side of the road because she had to vomit. But overall, going through those twelve days were without fanfare. The duration and dosage of radiation were minimal; Jae coasted through this stage of the process.

However, what proved to be difficult was that daily two-and-a-half-hour commute to and from the hospital. We had made the decision not to subject Jae to any more time away from home than was necessary. This meant waking up at three in the morning, bundling her up because it was cold, and driving through the dark for the appointment. The benefit of making this decision was that we were normally done with everything by 8:15. So, the time at the hospital was not an issue. I loved the idea of getting back home no later than noon and enjoying the rest of the day around the people we loved. My body got used to the early morning wake-ups. Jae normally slept through getting bundled up and the drive to Gainesville. But during this time, I felt alone.

Since Dee was the newly-minted county manager, and my career allowed more flexibility to be away, it was my responsibility to take Jae to Gainesville every day. Also, it was my responsibility to care for her during the day. As a public figure, I had grown accustomed to being seen in and around the community. Whether championing a cause or providing the community with needed resources, I enjoyed being around people and being an influencer. Taking on the sole responsibility as Jae's caretaker, stripped me of the life I had grown to see as normal. I wouldn't dare insinuate doing anything for other people was more important than what I needed to do for my child. But not seeing my wife until six or seven in the evening, and having to do all of this by myself, began to take its toll on me. I was privileged to be in the position to dedicate all of my time to Jae. Still, it didn't mask the fact that I was lonely most of the day.

As Dee continued to rise in her aspirations, I drifted further and further into an abyss, where my existence seemed to only be that of Jae's caretaker. Warranted or not, I felt forgotten, underappreciated, and useless to the world. This was especially hard when I had been so significant before. But now, my only significance was taking care of a two-year-old, who only wanted to watch "The Princess and the Frog" a million times a day.

Those feelings of loneliness began sinking in as I'd leave Dee asleep in the bed, knowing she was about to start a normal person's day while I traveled alone through the dark on a deserted highway. I know it's unsafe to text and drive. But on one dark morning, as I drove, I felt lonelier than I ever had. God began ministering to me.

On January 17, following the receipt of much-needed revelation, I started typing a message I later posted to Facebook, nce Jae went back and started her eighth day of radiation.

Traveling at 4 AM is a totally different experience than traveling in the middle of the day. That's what I've been doing the last two weeks, and I can tell you that traffic is very light and it's terribly dark, especially on 1-10. It's also a very lonely ride, considering that Jae normally sleeps the whole way to Gainesville. Due to the darkness and the loneliness ... I always perk up a bit when I see other cars on the road. Because it's so dark, even with my headlights beaming, driving through the darkness becomes easier with more lights shining on my path.

This morning, something happened that I hadn't ever experienced before. Even though traffic is always very light, there's always a car in front of me or behind me ... even if in the far distance. But this morning, I encountered a stretch of road where I couldn't see another car in front of me or behind me. You talk about dark and lonely .... for those 5 minutes, it was very dark and very lonely. God begin to speak to me in that moment.

Life is always easier when you can see and feel people around you, especially during dark times. But there are times, even though you know others are in the not so distant vicinity, that you begin to feel like no one's there. I've been there a few times over the past 7 months. But this morning when I didn't see any cars in front of me or behind me ... I kept thinking ... there are going to be lights at some point soon ... maybe just around this next corner ... because I know there are people just like me on this road too. If I keep driving, I'll run into them after a while.

My Word for you today is ... It may be dark right now ... but keep moving forward. Your lonely days will soon be over. But until then, work with the light that you have ... knowing it works when people are around, and it also works when nobody's there. That Light is Jesus, and He shines bright at all times. Lean on HIM while you wait for human help and continue to lean on him after human help is found.

What I learned through those dark and lonely moments on the road was that sometimes dark and lonely moments are necessary for us to get to desired destinations. I finished those four days following that post with a greater sense of purpose and passion. It didn't matter anymore that I felt lonely. Truth was, I was never alone in the first place. God was with me; He guided and protected me every step of the way. Not only was God there, but my family and friends, who couldn't be physically present on most days, were also praying wherever they were in the world. Those were the prayers that took me from a dark lonely road to the place where now we all could see the light at the end of the tunnel. With chemotherapy, surgery, stem cell transplantation, and now radiation behind us, the finish line was in view.

CHAPTER 24
It's Getting Hot in Here

By the time we got to immunotherapy, the final stage of Jae's treatment plan, we entered into that phase thinking we had seen every possible thing there was to see as it related to side effects of the medications. We had been through chemotherapy and seen her vomit violently. We had gone through surgeries and seen her admitted to ICU for fevers. We had gone through stem cell transplantations and seen the horrible effects of mucositis, where she couldn't eat because swallowing made her feel like someone was scraping her throat with sandpaper. Stem cell transplantation also gave us experience with long stays in the hospital; we spent twenty-nine days in the hospital for that phase.

Though radiation was a breeze for Jae, waking up at three every morning for twelve days and driving the two-and-a-half hours back and forth to the hospital for treatment, proved difficult for us. We had seen the worst of this process and were mentally, physically, and spiritually prepared for this final stage. The doctors had disclosed that immunotherapy wouldn't be half as difficult as any of the other phases. So, we were prepared. There was an excitement about getting this last phase started. The finish line was in sight. In our minds, these next few months would be nothing more than a victory lap. Little did we know; this final round would test our faith like nothing else had since the first day Jae was diagnosed.

Immunotherapy, also called biologic therapy, is a type of cancer treatment that boosts the body's natural defenses to fight cancer. It uses substances made by the body or in a laboratory to improve or restore immune system functions. John Driggers even described it by saying, "It's like unleashing guard dogs to roam the body to protect it from future cancer cells that may try to return."

As with all of the treatments, we were warned about all of the possible side effects, including fatigue, fevers, nausea, vomiting, and shortness of breath. Prior to this phase, Jae had handled all of the other treatments like a champion and smiled her way through every side effect, even escaping some of the most serious side effects.

We had seen this little girl overcome everything she had faced. There was no doubt in our minds that her toughness would prevail again. When I called John, like I normally did before beginning a treatment phase, he made me think of some things that could have changed my positive outlook. Per usual, he gave me a much grimmer depiction of what would probably happen during immunotherapy. He had a frank way of telling us about his experiences in this process that often left us feeling and looking like we had seen a ghost. Due to how John made us feel during those conversations before he encouraged us that everything was going to be all right, Trevor and I came up with a nickname for him. He never knew this, but we called him the "Chief of Scare."

Though it scared me at times, I always took John's words and advice seriously. But I must admit, I always expected a little less to happen than what John said would happen. I especially took that approach when he shared that his daughter's fevers got so high during immunotherapy she had to be covered with ice bags to help keep her body temperature cool. I didn't say this out loud, but in my mind, I was thinking, "Seriously, John? Covered in ice bags?"

Much of what had been John's experience in this process hadn't been ours. But some of his family's experiences did match ours. Unfortunately, that whole covered in ice bags experience was one of the ones that matched. The doctors had cautioned us about the high fevers. They said to expect them as a sign that the immunotherapy was working properly. But not an ounce of that advice could have prepared us for the kinds of fevers we saw, and the things we had to do to cool her down. I should have taken John at his absolute word because Jae's fevers got so high that we had to pack her down in ice bags to keep her cool.

This wasn't necessarily a painful process for Jae. I'm certain she was uncomfortable, but these high fevers had me a little worried. Each time a doctor or nurse walked in, checked her vitals, and charted those fevers, running as high as 105, they always seemed confident everything was working as it should. After a few days, their lack of alarm was quite comforting. Asking for fresh ice bags and seeing my baby girl covered with them became normal to me. Immunotherapy started to get a little easier, but life started to get tougher. Not only was Jae's body temperature rising, but Satan was also about to turn up the heat on our personal lives.

CHAPTER 25
All Hell Breaks Loose

Earlier on in this book, I explained how perfect our lives were before we found out Jae had cancer. Our family was solid. Our careers were going strong. We were living in our dream home. Then, of a sudden, this bomb dropped in the middle of our perfect world and shattered it to pieces. By this time, our lives were far from perfect and quite uncomfortable, but we'd grown content with the state we were in, confident this particular season of trouble was about to be over.

We were in the final stages of Jae's treatment. She had responded remarkably to the process and was already cancer-free. In a few months, we were going to head back home for good to recover the bit of normalcy we still had after this year-long ordeal. Only the closer we got to the finish, the more difficult our collective lives became. If we had ever thought life couldn't get any worse for a family already in the deepest depths of the valley, we were sadly mistaken. Little did we know, there was no mercy for the weary. As we approached the end of our nightmare, a new one was about to begin. All hell was about to be unleashed on us again with such fury I started to question how much more could one family take. Like seriously, I felt like if one more thing happened to us, we were going to fall apart. And that one more thing kept happening over and over.

After being flattened by our baby's condition, we had managed to pull ourselves up. We had slowly started to pull what was left of our lives back together. What we had pulled together begin unraveling as we started the final of treatment. During one of our five-day stays in the hospital for immunotherapy, Dee went back home for work for a couple of days. She was the county administrator and had huge responsibilities, running a governmental office with hundreds of staff and serving the needs of five county commissioners. She had been doing a superb job, even though she had to do that job under the shadow of a child spending days on end in a hospital room battling cancer without her. She had been commended by local, state, and national officials for how she'd managed the county through crisis. A United States congressman, Senator, Florida's past and present governors, her staff, and four out of the five commissioners she worked for all said she was doing an admirable job. I knew she was doing a great job, too, and she was doing it under great duress.

I watched this woman cry time after time as she left Jae and me in Gainesville, grieving because she wanted to be with her child as she battled for life in a hospital room with tubes connected to her. But Dee knew that going to work and doing a good job was just as important as being with Jae. The reason was simple. Having her job meant our baby had the best health insurance and the best medical care. Without that insurance, there was no way we would have been able to afford the expensive treatments that ultimately saved her life.

One night while Dee was away at work and our daughter lay in that hospital room, this time with an extremely high fever, with her body packed down with ice bags, Dee sent me a text from her county commission's meeting simply stating, "They just voted to fire me."

I can't properly convey my emotions that night. I was shaken to my core once again. Here we were, still in the middle of the most difficult time of our lives, and we are dealt a blow jeopardizing our financial stability. But more importantly, jeopardizing our daughter's health. Dee's firing was more hurtful, because by and large, she had received rave reviews for leading the county well during her most difficult time, and for leading the county admirably through its most difficult time after Hurricane Michael struck our county as a Category 4 storm, leaving some dead and many homes destroyed. I can't stress enough that she was doing all of this as her two-year-old daughter laid in a hospital room fighting cancer. To make it worse, Dee lost her job primarily for political reasons. It didn't matter to them that she had done a terrific job. It didn't matter to them that our baby was fighting cancer. It didn't matter to them that Dee needed health insurance to ensure Jae could finish treatment.

For political reasons, three of the five commissioners heartlessly voted to fire her. Not only was it heartless, but it was also unimaginable considering their reasoning. County records of the meeting showed that two of the three commissioners, who voted for her firing, had glowing remarks for Dee after they cast their deciding votes. One even said Dee was smart and too important to the county not to have a position somewhere in the administration. Dee's firing was heartbreaking. It wasn't just heartbreaking for Dee and our family; the community was heartbroken, too. It felt bad that people I once counted as friends could do something like this when they knew what she was already going through and hadn't done anything to deserve being fired. Nothing about this made sense to us.

At the same meeting that Dee was fired, the county attorney was retained. What makes this important to note is that the majority of the commissioners had said this man had done a poor job; still, they kept him and offered him a probationary period. But Dee was terminated after the majority of the county commissioners said she had done a great job. She was entitled to an appeal, but those commissioners had already made up their minds. Losing her job was a foregone conclusion. As we waited for the final nail to be driven into her professional coffin, a few more daggers were being aimed at our lives.

CHAPTER 26
You Gotta Be Kidding Me

A midst Jae's second round of immunotherapy, one of our friend's grandmother passed away, and I was asked to eulogize her. I left Jae and Dee at the hospital on a Wednesday and was going to be gone until Friday afternoon. This would have been the day Jae was supposed to be released from the hospital for that particular round. However, that wouldn't be the case.

Shortly after I left the hospital, Dee called me and saying that Jae was being rushed into emergency surgery. Doctors had discovered a defect in the line connected to her bloodstream, which was used to get medications through her veins. This problem required attention and meant immediate surgery to fix the problem. We were ensured the surgery would be fairly simple. But the idea of having our daughter going through such a serious and unplanned operation, especially at the same time as Dee was fighting to keep her job, was a major setback.

I was torn up that I wasn't going to be there for my baby; I was growing weary over how quickly things had turned for the worse for us and how we had become evident targets of Satan's vicious attacks. "God, how much more do you expect us to take?" I yelled, driving the rest of the way home with anger brewing in my heart. I wasn't angry at God. But watching how horribly my wife was being treated by people I once called friends, compounded with a new problem to deal with in our baby's treatment, had me emotionally unraveled. I was angry about our life situation.

Soon as I arrived home, I received another call from Dee. When I saw her number flash across my cellphone's screen, my heart raced. It seemed like every call or text I had gotten from her over the past few weeks had been devastating news. From being fired to Jae's emergency surgery, it seemed like we couldn't catch a break. We were at the end of a long grueling process. We should have been celebrating all of the great things that we had seen God do. Yet, we were stuck in this dismal state where everything that could go wrong as going wrong. And the call I got from Dee on this particular day was no different.

She called to say that her grandfather, affectionately known to many as Deacon White, who had raised her, had been hospitalized for what doctors initially thought was a heart attack. But when he was admitted to the hospital, they found out he hadn't suffered a heart attack. Tests revealed he was suffering severe complications from having kidney stones. That was a huge relief for us and seemed like the break we needed. Going into surgery for kidney stones was a whole lot better problem to have than the initial prognosis of a heart attack. Combine that news with the news I later heard that Jae's surgery was a success and her treatment would only be delayed for one day; I went to sleep that night a bit more content than I was when the day began.

Early the next morning, the phone rang again. It was Dee, and she said, "Granddaddy is on life support, and doctors have called the family to the hospital because they don't expect him to make it." I was so numbed that I uttered, "You gotta be kidding me." The next morning, as I was on the way to eulogize our friend's grandmother, and Jae recovered from surgery, Dee called again and said, "Granddaddy just died."

Imagine this: *Your two-year-old daughter is diagnosed with stage four cancer. Your spouse is fired from a job that's needed so that your daughter can have health insurance and medical care. Then suddenly, the only man your mate ever knew as a father, goes into the hospital, has a successful surgery, only to unexpectedly die a day later. If this isn't what you consider the absolute worst seven months a person could have, you're not human; and you can't have any feelings at all.*

We were emotionally wiped out. What many people have viewed as our amazing strength in difficult times was sometimes what I called desensitization. So many bad things had happened to us that we had grown numb to the hurt that should have been associated with those bad things.

When I saw Dee face to face for the first time after her granddaddy passed away, she was emotionless. I was emotionless, too. We had no more tears to cry. We had no more feelings to release. We were empty. Going through all of the things we had been through over the past thirty days had made us awkwardly indifferent. It's not that we didn't care. We didn't have any feelings left in us to show that we cared; not about losing her job, not about losing health insurance, and not about the abrupt passing of her grandfather. The only thing we truly cared about was making sure Jae got through this process. We had come too far to be distracted now. But Satan had a few more attacks up his sleeves and being hardened by everything we had been going through eventually served us well.

Shortly after Dee's granddaddy passed away, my sister called saying that my own father, Clarence Sr., had been hospitalized. She didn't know precisely what was wrong with him. When he visited his primary doctor for a routine check-up, he seemed to be fine. However, his primary doctor had found a lump on my dad's neck that he wanted to get checked out. The only way to do all of the needed tests was to admit him to the hospital. We were in-between treatments when my daddy went to the hospital, so I went to visit him while I was home.

My mother had been upbeat about what was going on with him. Therefore, I wasn't too concerned about his hospitalization. As I exited the elevator on the floor where my daddy was, two words stuck out to me like a sore thumb that made my heart sink. Evidently, my mother had been keeping the whole truth from me. Those words were "Cancer Center." Yep, on top of my baby battling cancer, on top of Dee losing her job in the middle of our baby fighting cancer, on top of suddenly losing a man important to both of us, my daddy was diagnosed with throat cancer.

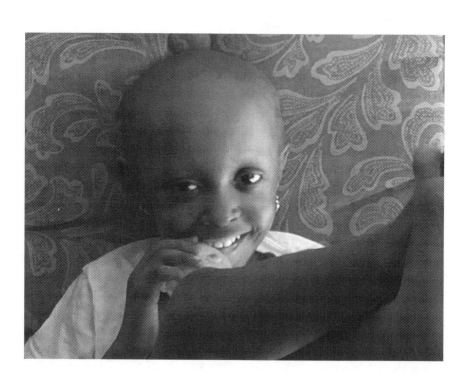

CHAPTER 27
And a Child Shall Lead Us

The worst eight months of my life had gotten worse. Not only had we lost Dee's job and granddaddy during this process, now I felt like I was about to lose my daddy. But more importantly than that, we lost our support system, too. All of the people affected by everything going on were the same people we had been leaning on through our time of crisis. Dee's mother was the person we called when we needed someone to keep Jae; now, she couldn't be there for us in that capacity anymore. She was dealing with everything revolving around the loss of her father, and she developed some health complications as well.

My mother and sister were the people who made sure our children and house were taken care of when we were away at the hospital, and they made certain we were fed and taken care of when we returned home. But they couldn't be there for us in that capacity because of everything revolving around my daddy's treatment and care. This was a time of great uncertainty, a time when we felt lost as it related to the great trials we faced and the great trials the people we held dearest were facing. Then my outlook changed when something amazing happened while we were at the hospital for Jae's fourth round of immunotherapy.

It was around three-thirty one morning; I woke up and noticed Jae was nestled right next to me. In a normal situation, that would have been a sweet occurrence. But this wasn't supposed to be happening. When I went to sleep, Jae was in her bed asleep, connected to everything from a heart rate and blood pressure monitor to an IV, carrying two immunotherapy drugs. Knowing there was no way possible for her to be in bed with me without being disconnected from at least one thing she vitally needed, I jumped up in a panic and called for the nurse. How she got out of her bed and made her way across the room over to my cot, turned out to be something mind-blowing, considering she's so young. And what she had done gave me the hope I needed to get through the rest of this fight, even amid all the tribulations that had befallen us.

What Jae had done was carefully disconnect the heart rate monitor from her foot and taken off the blood pressure cuff strapped on her arm. The nurse didn't immediately rush in when she noticed the disconnection on the screen at the nurse's desk. She figured I must have done it and could easily reconnect them when she came back for her hourly vitals check. It wasn't an emergency. In the dark and with no guidance from an adult, this little girl had neatly placed both of those monitors on the nightstand. But what she didn't do was unhook herself from the IV, pumping her medicine into her bloodstream.

Because of the rails on the side of her bed, I always got her out of the bed using extreme precautions. If one of those lines had gotten hung up on one of those rails while pulling her away from the bed, the results would have spelled disaster. She could have easily pulled a line out of her chest and neck, and blood could have rushed out of her body so fast that she could have died from the blood loss. But what she had done was managed to unhook herself from nonessential connections, carefully maneuvered out of her bed, and through bed rails without getting hung up, all to get to her daddy.

The nurse and I were shocked at what we saw. Jae had made up in her mind that she was going to do whatever it took to get to her daddy. She knew the stuff she could lose to get to me; she also knew the stuff she absolutely needed when she got to me.

Through this amazing happening, God showed me something powerful; it reshaped how we proceeded with the rest of this journey. Here it is:

If a three-year-old could do what it took in the dark to make it to her earthly father, there's no reason in the world why you can't do what it takes in the dark to make it to your Heavenly Father. Lose what you gotta lose and Get to Me TODAY!

Jae's mission to get to me had shown me how important it was for me to do whatever it took to get back to God. For whatever reason, Jae needed to get to me that night, and she did whatever it took. After witnessing this, I knew what I had to do. I had to get to God; I had to let Him take control again like I did when I let Him take control of my baby's healing. We had to put everything we were facing in God's hands and leave it there.

Immediately, I called Dee and shared the revelation. From that day forward, we proceeded with confidence. There was no way that God would bring us as far as He had brought us and let us see as many miracles as we had seen, to leave us now. From that day, nothing that was happening around us affected us to the point where we lost hope or felt helpless. God had shown us too much. If He had done it before for us, He was more than capable of doing it again.

God showed me something else just as powerful that strengthened my faith. There was one night when the machine carrying Jae's medicine started beeping, alerting that a cycle was complete. The nurse didn't immediately come in like she normally would. She took so long, and the beep got so annoying that I was tempted to press a few buttons and make it stop myself. Because I had been at the hospital and heard those beeps countless times and had seen what the nurses did when the machined beeped, I honestly felt I could stop it. I had been tempted on a few other occasions, to press a few buttons when the beeping went off. But I never did. Instead, I always waited for the nurse to come in and do what she was trained to do. Though tempted, I never touched that machine because I wasn't qualified. I never wanted to carry the responsibility of having to deal with the consequences if something malfunctioned. I didn't want to be the reason why Jae didn't get the absolute best care. Here's what God told me:

The same way that you have resisted the urge to touch these machines because of your lack of qualification is the same way you should resist the urge to touch those problems you have. Certainly, you can touch them if you want to. But it's not your responsibility ... that duty belongs to Me.

These revelations emboldened me. As I loosened my grip on our family's issues, I started to see God move mightily again, just as I had seen him move throughout this cancer battle. Honestly, this process and the situations we had faced along the way had been lessons on not having control.

Initially, it was the most miserable feeling I'd ever had. After all, how could anyone possibly enjoy being in situations they couldn't fix. But today, my lack of control was one of the most peaceful states I'd ever been in. I'd learned there were many things outside of my power, but nothing was ever outside of God's power. It was in those moments that I learned to rejoice in knowing God is always in control. He's in control of people, places, and things. Peace truly began to overtake me when I learned to turn all of my problems over to Him.

When we totally turned Jae over to God, He healed her body and let her go through a painful process with joy in her heart and a smile on her face. I would have been a fool by continuing to feel the way I was feeling, especially considering the best thing that ever happened in my life happened when I gave up control. I don't need it; I don't want it. I rest easy today, knowing that everybody and everything is under God's powerful hands.

CHAPTER 28

It is Finished

We started Jae's first round of immunotherapy on February 4, which was our twenty-second wedding anniversary. We started that five-day round knowing we were at the finish line, and it felt good. Though we had to celebrate this significant occasion in a hospital room, we were excited to have gone through this process, not looking or feeling like what we had been through. As Jae slept soundly nearby, we celebrated our wedding anniversary with an ordered dinner, under dim lighting, with sweet love songs playing in the background from my cellphone. I even broke all hospital protocol and slipped in a cheap bottle of wine into the room that we drank out of Styrofoam coffee cups I'd gotten from a hospital breakroom, just down the hall. We weren't in a fancy restaurant or an exquisite resort, but we were happy nonetheless, knowing we were celebrating our past together, and Jae's future with us. We were celebrating our history and her story. That night was great. We kissed. We slow danced. We enjoyed a truly special moment together with the place of our daughter's healing serving as the perfect backdrop.

Near the time we reached our final round of immunotherapy, we had gone through much more than we could have ever imagined. Yet we were excited, once again, to be at the end of this long road home. I'd be lying if I said we didn't crack under all the pressure we experienced, but we never crumbled.

On Memorial Day, May 27, we walked into Shands, knowing the last round of treatment was about to begin. We also knew by week's end; the yearlong inpatient portion of Jae's treatment would end.

Though we were understandably happy about this fact, there was less of a feeling of celebration than I had anticipated.

We had made elaborate plans regarding what we were going to do every day of that week. We had even decided to celebrate by doing something special each day to mark memorable moments we'd had over the time we'd been in the hospital. But, when that week was finally upon us, it was quite anticlimactic. I had wrapped my mind around the fact that we were about to be done, but we couldn't seem to generate the enthusiasm to match the occasion. Our baby had gone through nearly a year of grueling treatments, without any major complications or setbacks. Yet, our excitement was tempered down to the point that I dug deep to try to figure out why. After some deep thought about it, God revealed the reason to me.

God showed me that our moment of celebration had drawn the ire of Satan. The reason for everything Satan had done, in recent months, was an effort to steal our praise from us. Dee losing her job, and her grandfather and my daddy being diagnosed with cancer were all carefully orchestrated attacks aimed at our finish. The closer we got to the finish line, the greater the attacks we encountered. Satan knew we were close to a testimony that would change many lives. Therefore, his goal was to shut our mouths or fill them with so much bitterness that something as sweet as our baby's miraculous healing would be contaminated. But I woke up on the last day of Jae's treatment with a renewed sense of urgency to celebrate. It felt like it was her graduation date, and I was flooded with much joy. That Thursday morning, May 30, God put this poem in my heart, and I shared it with my Facebook friends:

When you get through the most difficult challenge
of your life, and the finish line is in view ...

Satan will throw every weapon he can, to try to distract you.

*But don't you dare lose focus ... he's shooting
because he knows you're close.*

*No weapon formed against you prospers ... no
matter how many arrows he throws.*

*The last challenge wasn't meant to stop you ... he
knew that stopping you wasn't in his hands.*

*He was trying to stop the CELEBRATION... because
he saw the VICTORY already in your hand.*

*Now you have a Testimony ... that Satan can't take
away. Move forward through the rest of life,*

knowing that God will always be with you every step of the way.

After that revelation, it seemed like the party had finally gotten started. From that moment, throughout that day, we were met with pleasant surprises. One of the sweetest surprises came as I was getting coffee from an atrium café. I gleefully grabbed my cup of Joe, turned around, and looked directly into the face of Dr. Islam, the surgeon who had removed 100 percent of the remaining tumor from Jae's abdomen. I don't know if he initially recognized me or how impactful he had been in my life, but that didn't matter to me. This was my opportunity to tell him, "Thank you," for what he had done. He greeted me with a handshake; I couldn't help but hug him. With God's help, he had performed a surgery that saved my daughter's life. I'll forever be grateful for him and his faith. As day turned into night and the remaining hours of medication flowed into Jae's body, more surprises were on the way. The countdown was on. The excitement was building.

Dee and I, gratefully watching each of the remaining drops of immunotherapy drip into Jae's veins. But watching those last drops by ourselves wasn't going to happen if Trevor Dunn had anything to do about it. A couple of hours before the medicines were finished, he and his two little girls burst through the door of Jae's room. His daughter Brooke was now just behind us in the immunotherapy process. Because of our connection, their visit was super special. Through us, they were about to watch and get a preview of the celebration that awaited them in a few weeks. Our finish was signaling the beginning of their finish; we were happy to share that moment with them.

After hanging out in the room for a while, watching the girls play, Trevor and I took a walk with an hour or so left in the treatment. We went down by the creek, where we had spent so many dreary days encouraging each other. But this time, we celebrated, reminiscing on our troubles, and rejoicing over how far we had come. When we got back to the room, he presented us with a bag and said he wanted us to open it when the last buzzer went off. Only we couldn't wait that long. We were so excited about seeing what he had brought that we asked him if we could open the gift right away. He obliged, and we did.

In that bag was a huge Florida Gators Flag, which was an evident poke at us. He knew we were Florida State Seminole fans and loathed the Gators. He brought it for all of us to sign and date it as a forever remembrance of this great day. Trevor also had what appeared to be a banner. I sat next to Dee on the bed as she held Jae. He unfurled that banner before us. It was white and had a huge purple cross emblazoned on it reading, "It Is Finished!"

As I was writing this, my eyes were filled with tears. It was a powerful moment that gives me chill bumps until this day and probably will for the rest of my life. I had held my emotions in check for most of the day. But seeing this and understanding what it meant, brought forth a flood of tears. They were joyful tears, though. Dee and I were overwhelmed with joy. Shortly following that special moment, we received another surprise. John and Jenifer Driggers and all of their children slid into the room. Their daughter Juliana had already gone through this process, and this family had been the visible evidence we needed to be confident we could get through it, too.

With about thirty minutes left until the last drop was scheduled to drip, all three families were together. There were elven people in that small room; it felt like we were having a party. This many people in one room was against hospital protocol. But all of the nurses and doctors knew how significant it was that all of us were together, so they allowed us this moment. As hours drew down to minutes, we all gathered around Jae and waited for that final beep. As minutes drew down to seconds, the mood in the room turned into somber reflections. Some of us wept, some of us hugged, but we all anxiously awaited the end of it all. With ten seconds left, I heard Jennifer say, "It's almost done." She began counting down, and we joined in with her. As we hit one, that buzzer went off. We celebrated as if we had all won the victory because we all had.

We couldn't have made it through this process without those people by our side. We will forever be grateful that all of them were able to share this special moment with us. After a long hard year, it was a great feeling knowing that this part of the process was done. All we had left now were a few final scans and ringing that damn bell.

CHAPTER 29
Things Are Changing

After immunotherapy, signaling the end of our long year of hospital stays, life started feeling normal again. We didn't have to worry about fevers in the middle of the night, usually meaning an ambulance ride back to Gainesville and another week in the hospital. We didn't have to worry about Jae experiencing pain or other side effects that often made our stays at home feel more like an extended stay at the hospital. For the first time in a while, we were free from it all, and it felt grand. Outside of a few more weeks of oral medications, we were living free and enjoying catching up on all of the time we missed being together as a family, reconnecting to our friends, and readjusting to being home for good. We had parties and family get-togethers for no reason. We sat under the veranda and listened to music all day without a care in the world. I eventually started to get back into the swing of life without the strain of being a caretaker. Doors of opportunity started to open for Dee so fast she had to tell potential employers to give her time to spend with Jae before she made any decisions. It was amazing to see how God had turned everything around so quickly for us.

Throughout this time, we were celebrating a series of "lasts." We celebrated my daddy's last round of chemotherapy and radiation and him being declared cancer-free. We went back to Gainesville and celebrated with Trevor and Brooke as she finished her last round of treatment the same way they had celebrated with us. We celebrated Jae's last dose of oral medications on a night when family and friends just so happened to already be gathered at the house. Then, we celebrated the last time Jae would have to go to the local hospital to get her patch changed, a weekly ordeal that was always difficult due to the discomfort we'd often have to see Jae endure. By that last visit, the end was right before us. That next Tuesday, July 23, we made another early morning trip to Gainesville for final scans.

Going back to the hospital for scans and even ringing the bell, had oddly been something we hadn't spent much time thinking or talking about. We were enjoying our new life, free from the rigors of cancer treatment. We had made no elaborate plans, and as that day approached, we were happy knowing we were at the finish line, even if that meant we would stand there alone, minus all of the fanfare we always thought would be associated with such a great day. Although we had nothing planned, it turned out that God and the people who loved us had already made plans for us. We didn't anticipate any fanfare, but fanfare was in order, and it was definitely on the horizon. Before we were able to stand under that bell we'd been dreaming about for a year and a month, Jae would have to lay under two machines that would tell us if she was ill cancer-free.

That Tuesday, we arrived at Shands around eight in the morning for an 8:30AM appointment to begin the process. At that appointment, Jae was injected with a dye that would light up the screen if any cancer was still in her body. That scan was scheduled for later that day around one. As we waited for the dye to work inside of her, we took Jae over to have her CAT scans done. After about twenty minutes for CAT scans, we went to have breakfast at a local restaurant where we were greeted by the owner, who asked why were we in Gainesville. He asked because he had never seen us before. When Dee explained Jae's triumph over cancer, and how we would be ringing the bell the next day, he tearfully told us about his family's battle with cancer.

He wanted to take a picture with Jae and said he would hang it in his restaurant to serve as inspiration for him and any other family that might pass through his doors with a similar story. Later, he presented Jae with a sweet treat he made specifically for her as a reward for being "such a brave little girl." As Dee was talking about Jae's triumph over cancer, I was silently wondering if the scanning process we had begun earlier in the day would tell the same story.

While we passed the time, waiting on our one o'clock appointment, my anxiety level rose a bit. I wasn't scared about the results as much as I was anxious about the wait we'd have to endure to get the results. I had a pretty good feeling the scans would prove what we already suspected. But I got to admit that the idea of waiting on that proof to show up on those scans and hearing it confirmed by the doctor, was quite an ordeal. When we returned for the appointment, I walked Dee and Jae back to the scan room and left to wait for their return. After about forty-five minutes, they reemerged from the double doors, and we were off to our friends Greg and Paula Archie's home in nearby Hawthorne, where we were staying for a restless but exciting night before the big day.

CHAPTER 30
A Chapter Closed?

T he next morning, we woke up early, had breakfast with Greg and Paula, and got dressed for the big day. The final scans were to take place that morning, followed by a crucial meeting with Dr. Lagmay. If those scans showed Jae was still cancer-free, we would be ushered to that beautiful shiny gold bell to finally ring it. There was also a mandatory bone marrow scan Jae would have that day. But that bone marrow scan would take place after we got the results of the other scans. There wasn't much concern from the doctors about doing that scan after the bell ringing. Typically, the bone marrow scans mirrored the results of the other scans. So, we had no worries about doing that test after the fact. Our primary focus was on these primary scans and their results.

That morning, unlike the many days I had gotten dressed in the hospital, I dressed up in a full suit. It was the same classic blue suit and red tie I always wore when I meant business. I chose to wear a suit because, for the past year and a month, hospital doctors and staff had only seen me in t-shirts, sweat pants, and FSU ball caps. Choosing to wear a suit, symbolized the dramatic change that was happening and the fact that my life was about to go back to normal. Dee was dressed beautifully, as usual, in a classy blue dress; Jae was decked out in a personalized shirt gifted to her by family friend Brittani Stokes with the words "Cancer Picked the Wrong Girl" emblazoned across it.

We were ready and excited. Before we left for the hospital, I walked into the bathroom to look in the mirror one last time. When

I looked in the mirror this time, tears begin to flow uncontrollably down my face. I was a bucket of emotions. I was happy for this nightmare to be coming to an end, but I was also thankful we had gotten through this process together without experiencing most of the adverse things that could have happened. Looking at my teary eyes in that mirror also reminded me of all of the days I had slipped away to the bathroom to cry alone, hiding my pain from my family. But I finally pulled my self together enough to walk out of the bathroom. I was still a bucket of emotions, but I wasn't crying. I gathered my girls, and we left for the hospital.

When we got to the hospital for the last scan, everybody noticed how well dressed we were. Many people asked what the occasion was, especially since many of them knew I never dressed this way. We also stuck out like sore thumbs because a camera crew, documenting the bell ringing, was following us around. When we finally made our way to the ground floor for the scans, I did as I had done the morning before. I walked Dee and Jae back to the scanning room and waited, just outside those double doors, for them to return.

While waiting for them, I received a call from my sister. She said that my mom and my dad had come down with her so they could share in the celebration. This was especially good news because my dad had been weakened by his bout with cancer. We didn't think he would be able to make that trip, even if he wanted to. Hearing her voice and knowing they were at the hospital to share in this moment caused all of those emotions that were bubbling up on my insides to resurface.

My sister brought a beautiful cake for the celebration and other sweet treats that were donated by Kimmie Kakes, a wonderful bakery from back home. As I was talking to her, I left the ground floor where Jae was receiving the last scan to meet them in the hospital atrium. By the time I got there, they were already sitting down. They didn't see me before I saw them, but from a short distance, I cried. Thoughts of knowing how much we all had been through and knowing we had overcome it all, started a flood of emotions that gripped me and wouldn't let go.

Shortly after greeting my family in the atrium, Dee called to say that the scans were done. They were headed upstairs to the fourth floor to meet with the doctor to go over their findings. My heart was racing rapidly; I felt out of breath like I had been running a marathon or something. Gasping for air in excitement and anxious energy, I told Dee I would meet them at the doctor's office for the meeting. As I exited the elevator on the fourth floor, my nerves got the best of me. The same way I had never wanted to talk to the doctors before during treatments was the same feeling I had about talking to the doctor about these critical results. I didn't want to do it.

Instead of taking a right to go to the doctor's office, I took a left toward the wing of the hospital where Jae had received all of her treatment and that gold bell hang. As I stood at the door, undecided about whether or not to go in, some of the nurses saw me and excitedly told me to come inside. Their smiles, and the excitement exuded through them, comforted me a great deal. It was as if they already knew the results of the scans and were ready for the bell ringing to begin. So, I decided to walk through those doors. When I got close enough to that bell, I couldn't help but notice a huge difference in how the bell looked.

On any given day that I had passed that bell, I'd see it hanging there silently on the wall, waiting for its moment to be the star of the show. But on this day, the bell looked like it had been shined and prepped for a ringing ceremony. Typically, the bell stood alone, without anything hanging from it. Only today, a cord had been attached to the bell; it hung down just low enough so that we'd be able to reach up and grab it. I got chills as I stood there looking at it. It was as if the bell was speaking to me. I know this is going to sound super weird. But it was as if that bell was saying, "If I'm prepared and ready for you to ring me, why are you afraid to go see what the doctor says? Get over there and hear what the doctor says so that you can start the celebration with your family." At that moment, I left and scurried over to the doctor's office, knowing I had to have already missed the good news being shared.

When I entered the room, Dee was already inside. She was smiling, sitting in a chair next to the doctor, and Jae was in the corner playing with toys. I was expecting the atmosphere to be much tenser when I arrived. To my surprise, there was not an iota of tension in that room. Everybody in that room gleamed with excitement. Before I could get a word out of my mouth or take a seat beside Dee, Lauren, the ARNP, simply said, "Her scans were as clean as a whistle," and that was it. We were informed that the official bone marrow scan results, we'd do later that day, would come back in about a week. But any anxiety I had was immediately swallowed up by elation over finally hearing the confirmation of what we already believed.

By then, my phone was ringing off the hook! I was getting calls from family and friends saying they were at the hospital and wanting to know where they needed to come for the bell ringing ceremony. Dee and I were pleasantly surprised that so many of the people, who intimately knew our struggle, would be standing with us as the sound of that bell rang out through the halls of Shands Pediatrics 42. The sound of that bell ringing would signal the end to a process that had changed our lives forever.

As I was fielding calls and giving directions to the bell site, a crew of doctors and nurses walked in. They said that it was time to head over for the ceremony. I can't begin to tell you how excited I was now. It was as if a parade in our honor was about to begin, and Jae knew she was the Grand Marshall. I wish everyone could have seen the way she dropped her toys when they stated it was time for the bell ringing. That was so significant to all of us in that room because everybody in that room knew how difficult it always was to pull Jae away from her playtime. Usually, she had to be pried away from those toys, followed by a temper tantrum that lasted minutes. But on this day, she dropped those toys like they were hot potatoes, ran to the door, and led us down the hallway as onlookers cheered her on with congratulatory remarks. Jae knew that this was her moment.

Entering the doors, where the bell ringing would take place, the halls were filled with so many people. It was as if the successful end to this process meant just as much to the doctors, nurses, and other floor staff, as it did to our family and friends, who had surprised us by showing up. As Jae walked down the hall toward the bell, she received high fives and other heartfelt congratulatory encouragement.

While Dee and I walked behind her, we received tearful hugs of pure joy. Before we made it to the bell, I received a call from Dee's mother and a few other friends, who had gotten stuck on the elevator. They had been rescued just in time for the ceremony, so I walked back outside to meet them and ushered them in. By the time I walked back through those doors, the entire wing was abuzz. Jae and Dee were already standing under the bell like a groom would stand at the altar, waiting for his bride to walk down the aisle. As I approached them, I held back the tears. When I finally reached them, Dee and I held hands as Jae stood in amazement at all of the fanfare in her honor.

CHAPTER 31
I Couldn't Say a Word

The ceremony began with a corny song with the same tune of that old eighties Oscar Mayer hotdog commercial. You know the one that says, "My hotdog has a first name, it's O-S-C-A-R…" Though the song's tune was corny, the words were powerful and meant far more to us than they would ever mean to someone who hasn't gone through cancer treatment with a child. I don't remember the exact words, but between the phone call I made to Trevor to try to figure it out, and my recollection, I'm pretty sure this is the gist of the message the song conveyed. It went a little something like this:

Our Patient Has the Biggest S-M-I-L-E
Our Patient has the biggest H-E-A-R-T
We Love To See You Every day
But Now It Is Our Time To Say
Pack Up Your Bags, Get Out The Door
You Don't Need Chemo Anymore!!!

As the song concluded, a loud cheer erupted. I picked Jae up and kissed her, holding her tight. The smile on her face was as bright as the sun, and her energy matched that. She clapped when everyone else clapped and cheered when everyone else cheered. I noticed some of the nurses and other hospital staff shedding joyful tears. They must have been rejoicing over the fact that, just as they had never seen me in a suit, they had never seen Jae this vibrant, full of life, and so happy. They had only seen the weakened Jae, who was valiantly battling for her life while on those violent medications in those cold hospital rooms. Everybody was gleaming, and then it was time for Dt. Lagmay to make a speech.

She told the people standing around about Jae's remarkable journey and how Jae fought like few children she'd ever seen. She commended Dee and me for how strong we stood during this entire process, sharing how nurses often fought over who would care for Jae on shifts they'd work because we were such a pleasure to work with as a family. She presented Jae with an end of treatment certificate and a trophy that epitomized the champion she had been through it all. Her final words, in summary, were that she wished for Jae to live a long and healthy life so that she would become all she was destined to be. And then she looked at me and said, "Daddy, would you please share a few words?"

Throughout this ceremony, I had kept it all together. From the time I cried, just before meeting my sister and my parents, I had been solid, or at least I had the appearance of being solid. But this whole day, my emotions were boiling like soda that had been shaken in a bottle. When she looked at me and asked me to speak, that bottle top came off, and all of those emotions just poured out. God knows I tried to pull myself together; there were so many things I wanted to say. For some reason, I couldn't, even as my family and friends encouraged me. As I wept uncontrollably, causing many people in those halls to weep with me, I finally came to the conclusion that I wasn't strong enough to utter a word. So, I turned to Dee and nodded, acknowledging I was giving her the floor. Dee was much stronger than me. After wiping away a few tears of her own, she was able to convey her message of gratitude. Among other things, she praised God for all He had done, thanked the doctors and hospital staff for how amazing they were during this whole process, and our family and friends for their steadfast support.

At the conclusion of Dee's speech, Dr. Lagmay stated that the moment we had been waiting for over a year, and the moment I had prophesied would happen from the beginning, was finally here. It was time to ring that "damn" bell. I picked up Jae again, and the three of us grabbed that cord, took a few deep breaths, and with cheers from our family and friends, we rang that bell as loudly as we could. The ringing sound that emanated and bellowed through those halls, along with the sounds of tears and cheers from everyone standing around, combined to be the sweetest sound I had ever heard in my life. I truly wish I was able to verbally express what I felt that day, especially at that moment. But my not being able to speak didn't dampen the celebration one bit. There was a party taking place, and it served as hope for every child lying in the hospital rooms on that floor and for every parent anxiously sitting by their sides. We had become a symbol of hope for them and proof that with God's help, even cancer can't stop a miracle from happening. For us, the process was over. But our finish, represented for all of those other children and families still in the fight that they were going to finish, too.

If I were able to speak that day, here's what I would have said:

When we found out Jae had cancer, our world was shattered. Initially, I couldn't see why God would allow something like this to happen to our baby. But though I would have never chosen this journey, at this point, after seeing how mightily God has moved, I wouldn't change it.

Dr. Lagmay, I want to thank you and your amazing team. From the beginning, you provided us with an assurance that we were coming out of this. Your smile and your hugs gave us confidence in your capability and was that was central to the confidence we needed to believe that our baby was going to be fine in your care. You never made us any promises other than to promise that you were going to do your absolute best to give Jae the best chance to live. Your best was more than good enough. You are truly a gift from God. This hospital, these children, and their families are blessed to have you. We are their witnesses.

To Dr. Islam, you showed us your faith in God. Right before surgery, you said, "If God is willing, I will get all of the cancer," and you also said, "I don't believe God has brought us this far not to finish what He started. I will never forget those words nor the moment you called me with the best news I had ever heard. We will forever be grateful to you.

I want to also thank every one of these nurses. You dealt with our baby as if you were dealing with your children. Your care for us was evident from day one. You became our family away from home, and you even met needs we had that couldn't have been in your job description. For this, we will be forever grateful.

To Mrs. Davis, our janitor, seeing your face every morning brightened some of our darkest days. To some, you're just the lady who cleans the rooms and takes out the trash. But to Dee and me, you are a friend who encouraged us every time we saw you. Don't ever minimize your value. What you've done for us far exceeded our expectations. You made our experience here a wonderful one, and we will forever be grateful for you.

To our family and friends, you all made this journey so much easier than it would have been had you not been there. There's no way we could have done this without your steadfast love and support. We are truly blessed to have you in our lives. I'm looking forward to spending more time with you and showing each of you just how important you are to our lives.

To Trevor and John, you guys were my rocks. Never once did you let me slip into unbelief. Consistently, you encouraged me and pushed us towards our finish. Cancer did for us what our mothers couldn't... It made us brothers. I'll forever be grateful.

To our children, you guys proved to be so strong throughout this journey. The way each of you excelled academically and took on new responsibilities with grace while going through this difficult time is remarkable. You made our lives so much easier by not giving us any more reasons to worry.

To Dee, you were an amazing partner throughout all of this. I'm amazed by your strength. Not only did you care for Jae during this time, but you also cared for me in a way that lifted me. I've always known I was married to a great woman. Now I know I'm married to Super Woman.

And to Jae, thank you for being brave, baby. Thank you for smiling on days I know you were in pain. Thank you for making me feel like you were okay on days I know you must not have been okay. You are our champion. You are our example of how each of us should take on the challenges of life with grace. You're going to live a long life and tell the story of all that God has done for you.

Lastly, I want to thank God for displaying His power in this situation. We will forever glorify You for being a way maker and a promise keeper. You did this, and You deserve all of the glory and the honor.

CHAPTER 32
Hold Up, Wait a Minute

After the bell ringing ceremony and a festive reception at the hospital shortly thereafter, we went out for a private dinner with a few of our closest family and friends. The atmosphere was celebratory; it felt like a weight was finally lifted off of our shoulders. That feeling traveled with us back home later that day, too. Knowing this process was over, felt similar to a graduation from high school or college. All of the tests that stood in the way of graduation were passed, and the bell ringing was like walking across the stage to receive the diploma we had earned. Dee and I could finally rest easy. Nothing related to Jae's medical journey, not even the fact that we hadn't gotten the official bone marrow scan results, hung over our heads.

We weren't worried about those scan results because the other scans had come back clean. From all indications, and based on her doctors' comments, our confidence in the favorable results of the bone marrow scan was reinforced. After all, they certainly wouldn't have let us ring that bell without having the results, especially if they weren't convinced those scans weren't going to yield the same "Cancer Free" outcome. So, we waited without any anxiety or fear.

In our minds, it was a forgone conclusion as to what they would be. Then on one Tuesday morning, I was on my way back from distributing food to the needy at our church, Dee called me, and her tone of voice was grim. That's when Dee said that she had just received a call from the doctor; the results of the bone marrow scan were not as clean as any of us expected. The doctor said that there was less than one percent of Jae's bone marrow that was abnormal and consistent with signs of a return of the cancer. Wait a minute! What? Yelp, her bone marrow scans had come back abnormal enough for us to fear that Jae's cancer had returned.; which would've been totally unprecedented.

I can't begin to articulate how deep my heart sank regarding that news. I heard the sadness in Dee's voice, and I had to get home immediately. When I got there, our house was cold and already filled with gloom. All we did was stare at each other in disbelief. She'd later tell me the doctor also said that it was highly unlikely the cancer had returned that quickly, and the other scans should have picked it up. Still, none of that was any consolation to us. We were immediately advised to restart an oral cancer-fighting medication and to head back to the hospital in a month to redo the bone marrow scan to be certain of this abnormal finding. I couldn't believe this, and I was angry—not fearful or anxious, but mad as hell that they would let us walk across the stage, get our diploma, only to tell us after the fact that we had to go back to summer school. Why in the world would they let us celebrate a bell ringing, only to tell us a week later that we might have to start this process all over again?

I was angry for days, not at God, but at the doctors and medical professionals who had encouraged us to celebrate what became a "false finish." I was so mad I even contemplated not going to the bell ringing ceremony of little Brooke Dunn, who was scheduled to celebrate her finish before we were scheduled to head back to the hospital to get the new bone marrow scans done. We were shaken, just as we were on the day we found out Jae might have cancer.

This time, we didn't tell either of our families what was going on. We couldn't bear telling the people who had just celebrated with us a week earlier that Jae might still have cancer in her body. We hid this new revelation from everyone except Trevor Dunn and the Driggers family. They were the only people we trusted with this information; each of them had experienced setbacks in their treatment processes. Therefore, we knew we could count on them to process this information without losing their minds.

When I told Dee that I didn't want to go to Brooke's ceremony, our outlook about all of this shifted. Dee chastised me for the thought of not being there for Trevor and Brooke, especially when Trevor had always been there for me. She reminded me of how Trevor had stood and celebrated when I received the news that the doctors were able to get 100 percent of Jae's cancer during surgery, even though he had just gotten news that his daughter's cancer wasn't responding as well to treatment and surgery hadn't gone as well as they had hoped. When Trevor celebrated with me, he had just gotten the news that Brooke would have to go through an extra round of chemo, meaning we would leapfrog them in the process.

Her words were, "The same way that God turned Brooke's situation around after they praised God for our good news is the same way God is going to turn our situation around because we celebrate with them in spite of our bad news." She continued, "God's name is on the line. There is no way that God would allow Jae to have such a public, miraculous healing, only to turn around and have her testimony destroyed." That was the turning point. Dee had forcefully ushered me back to the same type of faith that had brought us from Jae's diagnosis to this point.

From that moment, we began holding God accountable for what He had told us about Jae's healing, and we walked in faith. We believed the next results we'd hear would be the results we needed to hear. From that day, we went on about our daily lives, living our new normal. I was ready to get these scans over with already. But we didn't let this setback keep us from believing God was setting us up for another celebration.

We were living carefree again. So carefree that we didn't even cancel our big plans to have a few of our friends in town for Labor Day weekend to attend a much anticipated "Southern Soul" Concert being held in our city. Going to this concert was especially exciting because, it was going to feature some of the artists that we normally listened to on our long rides to and from the hospital; Tucka and Calvin Richardson being two of Jae's favorites. Scheduling this concert was huge considering that the new bone marrow scans were slated to be done just three days before the concert.

On Tuesday, August 27, Dee took Jae back to the hospital for the bone marrow scans. I didn't travel down to Gainesville for the scans, opting to stay at home with the kids, who had just started back to school. I also needed to take care of some pastoral responsibilities.

By Wednesday, August 28, the entire process was over. Dee and Jae were back home later that day. All that was left now was to get the call from Dr. Lagmay and listening to the results. We knew it would be one or two days before we received the call, and we also knew that the call could come as several of our friends stayed at our house before, during, or after the concert. But we didn't change our plans.

We heard nothing on Thursday, August 29, which wasn't shocking. As our friends started to arrive on Friday, August 30, for the concert and a pre-planned, fun-filled Labor Day weekend, we had heard nothing. Around four in the afternoon, we all left the house to head over to the concert venue. By the time we arrived, we still had heard nothing. When we pulled into the parking lot, I asked Dee to call the doctor's office to see if the scans had been analyzed and if the results were ready for us. I was growing a bit impatient. The thoughts of when that call might come through and what the doctor could say had begun clouding my mind. Truthfully, it was interrupting the good thoughts I had of having a good time. Dee must have been feeling the same way, because she didn't hesitate to make that call. However, when she called, one of the doctor's assistants said that the scan results weren't ready and that there was a high likelihood we'd have to wait until Tuesday for the results, considering the three-day weekend due to the holiday.

Both of us had been over-confident about the outcome of the bone marrow scans. After hearing we would have to wait longer for the results, our moods shifted a bit. Anxiousness had slipped in, and stress manifested itself on our faces. A million questions raced through my mind, including, "Does this mean they are preparing to give us more bad news? Does this mean they want to prepare a new treatment plan before they deliver the news?" My mind had automatically been drawn to the worst of thoughts. I was trying to figure out what did this delay truly mean? But we couldn't let any of our emotional distress show. We had friends in town for a concert; we needed to mask any feelings so that we could show them the good time we had promised them. After all, they had no clue about what was really going on. So, we pulled our emotions together, got out of the car, and marched into the concert with Jae in tow. Yes, I said with Jae in tow.

Even though children weren't supposed to be allowed in, we had gained special permission from the concert promoter to bring her. We wanted to bring her because whenever we'd be sitting under the veranda listening to music, she'd always get up and dance whenever either of the two featured artists' I mentioned earlier, blared through the speakers. We knew Jae would love being in this atmosphere, and it would be an occasion we'd remember for the rest of our lives. This was supposed to be a good day. When we initially planned on going to this concert, we considered that this would be an amazing way to celebrate the successful end to our long year fighting cancer. After ringing the bell, this would be our way to continue the celebration. Now there was a dark cloud looming over what was otherwise a beautiful day.

Before the concert began, I took the stage to do an opening prayer; I had been asked earlier by the concert promoter to do the pray after he learned of our plans to be in attendance. After the prayer, I made my way back to where Dee and Jae were sitting to ask if they wanted anything to eat. They did, so I went to the top of the hill, where the food trucks were, to place an order. As I stood in line, and the bands began to play and sing, my phone rang, and it was Dee. I was thinking maybe she was calling to change her order. But when I answered the phone, she said, in a rather melancholy tone, that the doctor had called. In a panic, I yelled, "What? What did she say?" The tone of her voice and the negative thoughts already in my mind caused me to fear the worse.

Knowing that I must have been about to lose my mind, she abruptly shifted to a more excited tone and yelled, "Boy, calm down! The scans came back clean!"

Hearing this news, I let out a shout so loud that everybody near me could tell I had just received great news. The sounds of the music filling the amphitheater was sweet to my ears. The cloud had lifted, and this concert had all of a sudden become an even greater celebration. God had done it again. We turned that concert into our party, dancing and singing the night away with our baby girl, who danced and sang like she knew that she was once again declared "Cancer Free! What an amazing way to end a truly amazing long road home.

"...Your life can go from flipped upside down to being flipped back to right side up in a matter of moments. Just hang in there long enough to see how God SHIFTS It. He's GONNA Do It!"

Unedited post to Facebook on October 1, 2018

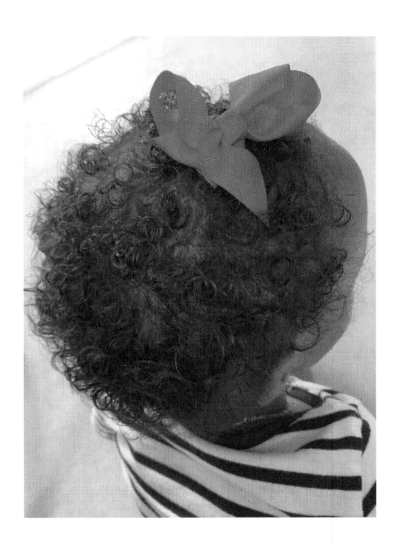

CHAPTER 33
Our New Normal

By the time you read this book, much of our lives, would be back to normal or as close to normal as it could possibly be; considering that we will spend the next five years going back to Shands for follow-up visits to ensure that Jae is still cancer free. But for us, that reality is small in comparison to the fact that we no longer live with the dread of a cancer diagnosis or the rigors of an aggressive treatment plan. If this is our new normal, we gladly accept it; knowing that our baby girl is healthy and happy and more vibrant a child than we had previously known.

Things are looking up for all of us now. Just one month after Jae finished treatment and rang the bell, she was enrolled in school. I had worried about how so much time away from school and other children would affect her. I also worried if she would be able to emotionally handle not being around me or Dee everyday all day. Truthfully, I worried about how I would handle sending her off to school and not being with her everyday all day. But those worries quickly subsided on her first day of school.

Jae walked into that classroom as if she was excited to get her new life started. Initially, I was broken up about leaving her there. But hearing the details of her successful first day put my mind at ease. Today Jae is excelling in school; testing among the highest scholars in her class on tests and socializing without any problems. She's blossomed into such a confident and inquisitive child who enjoys her little life to the fullest. She loves music and dancing. She loves standing in the mirror acting out her favorite scenes on TV shows and movies. She loves being outside and exploring the wonders of nature just like me. She loves going to school. She loves life.

Just months after she rang the bell, Dee and I took Jae, Jan and Joana to Disney World; Jaelen was had started a new job a needed to be at work. The highlight of that visit was when Jae got the chance to meet Princess Tiana of Princess and the Frog. Remember, Jae watched that movie almost every day; several times a day. When she walked into that room and saw Princess Tiana she put her hands over her face in disbelief that she was actually in her heroin's presence. Even the princess wept after Dee told her about Jae's journey and explained why Jae was so emotional about seeing her. Jae wept, not because she was sad but because of the immense joy and exhilaration she was feeling at that moment. That day we made many great memories, And that's exactly what we plan to do every time God affords us such quality time.

After her treatment plan ended, I often thought of how difficult it would be for Jae to be reintegrated into society after all of those days at home and in the hospital. But, this new normal has proven not to be a challenge for this bossy and feisty little girl. The same way she valiantly faced and defeated cancer is the same way she's valiantly facing life and winning each day with a smile on her face. She's still an inspiration for so many and she seems to know it. She gracefully wears her crown as a princess warrior who continues to prove that there's no trial she can't triumph.

After months out of work, Dee finally started to explore job opportunities. What she found was that there were many people who admired how she handled herself during the many trials she faced during Jae's illness. They also admired the work portfolio that she had compiled in her previous line of work. Because of who she is as a person and employee, support from potential employers poured in. At the time this book was published, Dee had received several offers to return to the workforce and was weighing all of the opportunities she'd be favored with. What she chooses to do will ultimately revolve around making sure she will be able to spend quality time with her children and me. But greater than any of the amazing job opportunities she's been afforded, Dee has been vigorously working on another passion of hers; providing affordable housing for low to moderate income families. Today she operates Community Impact Partners; a nonprofit organization.

Our children, who we couldn't have been more proud of; considering how gracefully they endured this process, are all excelling as well. In the spring of 2020, our oldest son Jalen is graduating from Florida A&M University School of Business and Industry with dual degree including a master's degree in Business Administration; specializing in finance. He's also been employed by Wells Fargo Bank with pending employment opportunities from fortune 500 companies around the nation upon graduation.

Our daughter Joana is in her Junior year at the Florida A&M University School of Business and Industry. She's continued to excel academically as well. After Jae's diagnosis, she opted to come back home to help us out. I will be forever grateful that she made that choice because it allowed us to leave our youngest son in the comfort of his own home while we were away instead of being shuffled in and out of the homes of our family and friends. She commutes to school and is scheduled to graduate in 2021. After graduation she intends to go to law school to pursue a career in entertainment law.

Jan, our youngest son has always been the kid that we could count on to get in a bit of trouble at school. Though highly intelligent, as evidenced by his high test scores and excellent grades, Jan was always the child that gave us something to pray about. But, since Jae's diagnosis and subsequent healing, Jan has matured so much. He's more helpful than he's ever been around the house and he's the most tender big brother for Jae. Jan continues to do well academically and athletically. He's a sophomore at Crossroad Academy Charter

School where he is an honor roll student. He's also a six-foot three corner back for the Gadsden County Jaguars football team. He already being considered by some coaches as a Division 1 prospect, already garnering attention from some smaller schools eyeing him for athletic scholarship. Though athletic, Jan sees a future in becoming a Mechanical Engineer.

Our two families have seen quite the rebound too. Though we endured significant losses on this journey, one thing we didn't lose was our love for each other. Our connections have grown far stronger than they were before this ordeal. My dad is still cancer free and have returned to making his daily grocery store runs for my mother. He's also back to his regular visits to our house to see Jae and the other kids. He only wants to see me when it's time for me to cut his hair. But's that's all good. He's regained the weight he lost during treatment and at eighty-three years old, he looks and feels great.

My mom turned eighty years old in November 2019 and she doesn't look or feel a day over fifty. She's finally back to her weekly brunches with her friends. My sister Marsha is back to her busy travel schedule and seems to finally be getting a chance to enjoy her retirement. Dee's mom and sisters are well too. Her oldest sister Shalonda is getting married in a few weeks and we can't wait to be a part of yet another family celebration.

As for me, I'm taking life slow. I'm breathing a little deeper and gazing a little longer at things that use to pass me by when I was so busy being a man of the people. I'm enjoying being a family man. I take pleasure in being home when everyone else gets home and pulling out the grill to cook up steaks for impromptu parties we have for no reason other than being happy to be alive. I'm still a pastor, but I'm enjoying seeing other leaders emerge in ministry. Being gone for a year taking care of Jae showed me how capable some of my members were to carry loads that I'd previously carried alone.

At this time, I have no interest in reentering the political arena. However, I'm slowly reemerging as the community leader; this time with tempered expectations of myself. Life is good now. I wouldn't have chosen this life, but I definitely wouldn't change it at this point. Life for me has a richer meaning now. My priorities have shifted sharply. My Family has always been important to me, but now I see the value in spending quality time with them and making the most of every moment we have together. There are five specific things that this journey has taught me. Turn the page and I'll share.

THE END OF THE ROAD
Five Things This Journey Taught Me

ONE
God Can Do Anything

The most important thing I learned during this long, tedious journey is that God can do anything. I've been a believer for a long time. I thought I had faith in God already. But there was something about being in the darkest place I had ever been that made me trust God like I had never trusted Him before. I had no choice but to trust God. For the first time in my life, what happened next was completely out of my control. God proved to be able to defy the predicted occurrences and outcomes we were warned about and exceeded our expectations.

The fact that Jae is cancer-free isn't the miracle. The miracle is in how God kept her from what was supposed to happen and how He expedited the shrinkage of those tumors. The miracle was how a surgery that could have lasted eight hours turned into a thirty-minute operation. The surgeon said that it took longer to open and close her than it did to remove a tumor that had already released itself from vital organs. God, not medicine, caused that tumor to let my baby's body go and hate the fact it had attached itself to her. Dr. Islam said,

"It was almost as if the tumor was saying, come get me out of this girl's body." That was a miracle that only God could perform. What I know is that we all will face many trials in this life. But I also know now, that matter what we're faced with, God is faithful and can do anything but fail.

TWO

We Are Much Stronger Than We Think

About a week or so before Jae was diagnosed, I watched a St. Jude's commercial. I was thinking there was no way I could ever handle knowing any of my children had cancer. I often saw those commercials and felt so sorry for those children and parents. But I quickly learned that our expectation of what we can handle shifts quickly when we are forced to handle it. Dee and I have met people who have told us they don't know how we did it. My answer to comments like that were always the same, "You wouldn't have any problem doing it either if your child's life depended on you doing it."

We are much stronger than we think we are. But we never find out how strong we are until we are forced to handle the weight of a circumstance such as this. There were moments where we were not strong. In those moments, God did the heavy lifting so that we still appeared strong. We weren't always standing. There were many times that what looked like standing was actually God holding us up. We came out of this whole ordeal, not looking or feeling like what we had been through. When it matters most, we all will find that not having enough strength is not an option; getting through it is our only option.

THREE
Somethings Aren't Important

R ight before Jae was diagnosed, there was one thing bothering me. I was having a tough time getting my youngest son, Jan, to complete chores I had asked him to do. A little less than a week before we found out that Jae had cancer, I was furious that he had again "forgot" to take out the trash. I was so mad I didn't even speak to him for days and wasn't speaking to him on that fateful Sunday. I'm embarrassed now to say this was my typical behavior. I'd let my anger, even at my children, fester to the point where my relationships were strained. I was such a control freak and a worrywart. Not having a bill paid on the day it was supposed to be paid freaked me out, even with having at least a ten-day grace period on most accounts and plenty of money to pay them.

This diagnosis put what was important in life at the forefront of my life. All that mattered was my faith in God and the support of my family and friends. Nothing else mattered, not the trash being forgotten, not late bills, nothing! Sitting in that hospital, I realized I hadn't talked to my son in days, and the first thing he heard from me was something that shook his world to the core. I apologized to him. Today, the small things just don't matter. Today, I do my best to live each day with a focus on being happy and making the people I love happy.

FOUR
Savor Every Moment

Life is unpredictable. I can't tell you what the future holds for any of us. But what I do know for sure is that I will spend whatever time I have left on this earth, enjoying every moment I'm blessed to share with my family and friends. I've learned through this process not to look too far down the road; all we truly have is right now. I no longer dream about how many years I might live. Today, I only focus on the day in front of me. I do look ahead, but I don't look so far down the road that I start counting the days that might be on the way before I use the day currently in my hand.

The day after we found out Jae had cancer, Dee lamented the fact that on that Saturday before we went to the hospital, she was supposed to have washed Jae's hair. She put that off, thinking that she could do it the next day. Well, the next day never came, or at least it didn't come before all of her hair had fallen off of her head. Dee often cried about this, saying, "I should've washed Jae's hair while I had the chance."

The lesson in this is to do what we can while we have the chance. Trust me, in this life, we will encounter some things that will turn our lives upside down. It's wise to make the most of the moments when our lives are right side up.

FIVE

Trouble Don't Last Always

W hen the doctor first told me this process was going to last at least a year, I stared at her in total disbelief. Having to sit through only a few days of the process had already overwhelmed me. I asked, "Does that mean we will have to be in the hospital the whole time?" She responded, "Not the whole time, but you should be prepared to be here for most of that time."

I was standing straight, but everything within me crumbled. Jae had already had a difficult two days. How would she be able to handle a year of this, especially knowing this process would become more difficult before it would get better?

I received my answer when I called my mother to tell her about what the doctor said. Before I got the opportunity to express any of my fears about traveling this long uphill journey, she stated, "The only way to get through this is to take one day at a time." She also said, "Remember the words of my favorite song, trouble don't last always." Her words didn't comfort me much that day. But, as days turned into weeks and weeks turned into months, I started to understand what she meant.

There was no way to speed up life's clock so that we could get through this trial any faster. But what we could do was accept the reality that we must go through it and start taking steps to get through it. My focus was no longer on the end of the road, but the obstacles I was facing on the road. I resisted the urge to focus on the finish line. Instead, I focused on the step I was taking and the step after that. Before I knew it, those days turned into weeks, and those weeks turned to months, and those months turned into a year. Looking back, that long road wasn't as long as I first thought it would be; it wasn't as uphill as I had imagined, either.

ABOUT THE AUTHOR
Clarence Jackson

Clarence Jackson is a Pastor, Author, and Motivational Speaker. A Native of Gadsden County, Florida, Clarence is the Pastor of Destiny Church Tallahassee and Author of the book "The Day All Hell Broke Loose". He is a well-respected community leader and has served in elected office as Commissioner and Mayor of the City of Gretna, FL. He's been lauded for his passion for community outreach and has received many recognitions for his work, including an honorary Doctorate Degree from St. Thomas University, an appearance in the Tallahassee Community College Black History Month Calendar as well as being honored by then Florida Governor Rick Scott. He is married to Dee Jackson and together they share in parenting four children; Jaelen Allen, Joana Alexandria, Jan Adolphus, and Jae Alexia Jackson.

Printed in the United States
By Bookmasters